CAERPHILLY COUNTY BOROUGH

3 8030 08198 6450

M A O

Travel with
Insider
Tips

CYPRUS

NORTH AND SOUTH

TURKEY

GREECE

Istanbul

Nicosia

CYPRUS   SYRIA

Crete
(GR)   LEBANON

Mediterranean Sea

ISRAEL

EGYPT

P!

www.marco-polo.com

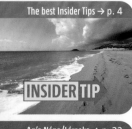

The best Insider Tips → p. 4

INSIDER TIP

Agía Nápa/Lárnaka → p. 32

Limassol → p. 44

Nicosia → p. 52

SYMBOLS

INSIDER TIP	Insider Tip
★	Highlight
●●●●	Best of ...
☼	Scenic view

☺ Responsible travel: fair trade principles and the environment respected

(*) Telephone numbers that are not toll-free

PRICE CATEGORIES HOTELS

Expensive	over 100 euros
Moderate	65–100 euros
Budget	under 65 euros

Prices for a double room with breakfast in the high season

PRICE CATEGORIES RESTAURANTS

Expensive	over 16 euros
Moderate	12–16 euros
Budget	under 12 euros

Prices are for a meat dish with side salad or a mesé platter (with 12 to 20 different items)

On the cover: Nicosia's architectural mix p. 52 | In the green valley of Agíi Anárgyri p. 70

CONTENTS

Páfos → p. 64

Tróodos → p. 76

North Cyprus → p. 86

CAERPHILLY COUNTY BOROUGH COUNCIL	
3 8030 08198 6450	
Askews & Holts	09-Apr-2013
915.693	£5.99
LIB1086	

DID YOU
Timeline
Local spe
Russians
Books & I
Cyprus' w
An icon a
Dazzling diversity
Budgeting → p. 117
Currency converter → p. 120

on the road atlas
(U A1) Refers to the map of
Nicosia inside the back cover

COVER:
AP →

... Refers to the
removable pull-out map
(𝕄 a–b 2–3) Refers to the
additional inset maps on the
pull-out map

The best MARCO POLO Insider Tips

Our top 15 Insider Tips

INSIDER TIP **Cypriot bohemia**

From the outside, the Art Café 1900 in Lárnaka seems nothing special, but don't be put off: inside, it has become the meeting point for the regional and international art scene – thanks to its excellent food and good wines as well as classic cocktails from the bar → p. 39

INSIDER TIP **Thank God for Britannia**

Lying as they do within the sovereign territory of the British military base, the beaches of Avdímou are not very well known. Which means, so far, they've not been spoilt by hotels and urban sprawl → p. 49

INSIDER TIP **Fresh ravioli**

At the Sedir Café in the courtyard of the former caravanserai of Büyük Han in northern Nicosia, all pastries are made by hand in front of the guests' eyes. Try the filled ravioli and top off the feast with honey yoghurt (photo above) → p. 59

INSIDER TIP **Market in front of the minaret**

Try and plan your trip to Nicosia for a Wednesday, which is when you can take in the large farmers' market on the medieval Constanza bastion on the city wall → p. 60

INSIDER TIP **The best mesé**

In the Laterna restaurant in Páfos, your host is committed to ecological winegrowing and is a passionate chef too. The wines for his guests come from small winemakers of the region → p. 68

INSIDER TIP **Living with artists**

In the hotel Kinirás in the Old Town of Páfos, paintings and frescoes by hosts and guests adorn the walls of the rooms and the secluded courtyard → p. 71

INSIDER TIP **Odysseus beneath the Ram**

The Classical sarcophagus of Koúklia was this millennium's first archaeological sensation. The find tells of the adventures of the hero Odysseus → p. 73

→ p. 73

INSIDERTIP **A village with history**

Modern art dominates life in what is today Lémba. The village's 4500 year-old predecessor, right next door and hardly visited, has been reconstructed → p. 74

INSIDERTIP **Top table**

In Pródromos, the highest village in Cyprus, enjoy a delicious Cypriot lunchtime buffet at the Byzántio restaurant, featuring a large selection of vegetables, meat, salads and local fruit and veg → p. 84

INSIDERTIP **Trout with garlic**

There's nowhere on Cyprus that serves a more delicious trout than the Mill Restaurant in Kakopetriá – without bones if you so desire, but always with garlic → p. 84

INSIDERTIP **Dune beaches**

At the small Balci Plaza hotel you are a stone's throw from the empty dune beaches of the Karpaz pen-insula, and have a lot of space to yourself (photo below) → p. 93

INSIDERTIP **White pearl**

Only at the White Pearl hotel do you get to enjoy the panoramic view of Kerýneia's port from your own balcony and live right on the harbour promenade → p. 95

INSIDERTIP **Village of palms**

In the village of Lefke in north Cyprus, hundreds of palm trees jut up against the backdrop of the Tróodos mountain range. Not many tourists venture this far → p. 96

INSIDERTIP **Babbling brook**

There are many hiking trails on Cyprus, but only the Caledonia Trail at Tróodos keeps crossing a stream, eventually leading to a waterfall → p. 111

INSIDERTIP **Classical music in the monastery**

For a whole month, famous virtuosi play classical music in Bellapaís Monastery between Gothic tracery and lancet windows → p. 113

BEST OF ...

FOR FREE

● *Concerts for free*
On nearly every Sunday in the year, Páfos, Limassol and Lárnaka host free concerts, sometimes folk or rock, sometimes jazz or classical. All events are organised by the relevant municipal authorities → p. 112

● *Where wishes (might) become reality*
Gain deep insights into Greek Cypriots' popular piety between the golden shimmering mosaics and expressive wall paintings of *Kýkko Monastery* and take up the invitation to look after your future at a wish tree. All this is still for free (photo) → p. 80

● *Under the mulberry fig tree*
Elsewhere on the island the place to see and be seen is the café; here in front of Lala Mustafa Mosque in Famagusta it's the 800-year old *mulberry tree*. Under its canopy you'll sit as if at the theatre, even saving your money for the mocha. At the purification basin in front of a Gothic façade pious Muslims undertake Islamic rituals, and school classes in uniform line up for the souvenir snap → p. 88

● *Freebie beach*
Many of the better beaches around Kyréneia/Girne in northern Cyprus charge a fee. For some free sun worship and a swim choose the pretty *sandy beaches* of Famagusta at Hotel Palm Beach and in front of the excavations of Sálamis → p. 90

● *Make art not accounts*
A bank building where the talk is not about accounts for once is the museum of the *Bank of Cyprus* arts foundation in Nicosia's Old Town. Stroll through 8000 years of Cypriot art history without having to pay a penny for the privilege → p. 54

● *Once around Mount Olympus*
The *Atalanta Trail* in Tróodos leads once around Mount Olympus: four hours as a free-of-charge nature trail. You don't have to be particularly fit, and there's no pub to require the services of your wallet → p. 100

●●●● Dots in guidebook refer to 'Best of ...' tips

ONLY IN CYPRUS
Unique experiences

● *Capital Cypriot meal*
In the taverna *Matthéos* in Nicosia's Old Town you can eat like the locals. Simple dishes like stew and sweet potato with pork are always accompanied by a platter of crudités and olives → **p. 59**

● *Folk dancing on the village square*
If you want to experience Cypriot folk dancing on a village square, head for the platía in Pissoúri to watch the authentic *folkloric* demonstration held once a week (photo) → **p. 51**

● *Cohabiting in no-man's-land*
One of the very few villages on Cyprus where Greek and Turkish Cypriots still live together is *Pýla* near Lárnaka. On the village square you have the choice between Greek-Cypriot and Turkish beer and can meet South American UN soldiers: Pýla, you see, is in no-man's-land → **p. 43**

● *Plenty of friends + plenty of dishes = a good dinner*
In the traditional taverna *Nápa* in Agía Nápa you can experience first hand how a true Cypriot dinner requires at least 15 different dishes on the table: from salads and tsatziki to calamari and lamb cutlets. And at least as many friends have to be seated around the table too → **p. 34**

● *Swimming near a ghost town*
Confront the brutal political reality at Palm Beach in Famagusta where you swim right next to a barbed-wire fence which, in 1974, turned *Varósha* into a ghost town → **p. 89**

● *Picnic in the forest*
At the weekend 'do as the Cypriots do' and pack everything you need for a delicious meal at one of the countless picnic sites in the north or south. Arguably the most beautiful lies in the forest of *Stavrós tis Psókas* → **p. 75**

● *Feast like a sultan*
Always wanted to feast like the Ottoman upper crust? Here's your chance: at the top nostalgic restaurant *Boghjalian Konak* in a historic merchant's house in northern Nicosia → **p. 59**

ONLY IN

BEST OF ...

AND IF IT RAINS
Activities to brighten your day

● *Cultural and culinary crossroads*
In the former *Carob Mill* in Limassol's Old Town, modern art and culinary delights from small ecological farms and enterprises meet hip bars, a microbrewery and restaurants with creative Cypriot cuisine → p. 46

● *A surfeit of museums*
At the *Archiepiscopal Palace* in Nicosia, five different museums lie so close together that your umbrella will hardly get wet on your way from one to the other (photo) → p. 55–57

● *Just dive down*
Use a day of bad weather for a trial dive offered by diving schools all across the island. The one at *Sunfish Divers* in Agía Nápa takes three hours and even on your first attempt takes you down to depths of up to 8m → p. 105

● *Dry shopping*
Instead of fruit and vegetables, meat and fish, the former *Market Hall* of Páfos now only sells souvenirs, albeit of all kinds. Viewing the huge selection takes time; take a rest in a simple market bar or café and think things over → p. 69

● *The pleasures of wine*
The *Cyprus Wine Museum* in Erími addresses all the senses. Eyes and ears will be treated to the interesting history and technology behind wine-growing on Cyprus, followed by an extensive wine-tasting session taxing the palate and the nose → p. 49

● *Model for a painter*
Theo Michael in Lárnaka is one of the best contemporary painters on the island. In his small studio in the Old Town he'll paint your portrait, in pencil or in oil, large or small → p. 39

RAIN

RELAX AND CHILL OUT
Take it easy and spoil yourself

● *Spa feeling in the historical hamam*
In the 400-year old *Omeriye Hamam* in Nicosia, Ottoman practices and contemporary requirements come together in harmony below the historical domes (photo) → **p. 57**

● *Revitalised healing springs*
The remote location in a green valley between Páfos and Pólis turn the *Agíi Anárgyri* resort into a luxury spa with a difference. The mineral water with healing properties not only feeds the pool but is also on tap in some of the bungalows and suites → **p. 70**

● *Lounging Indian-style*
In the *Moti Mahal* lounge bar in Lárnaka you can sit cross-legged on white cushions and slurp cocktails, enjoy curries and allow your gaze to wander across the ocean, surrounded by the scent of incense sticks and accompanied by the sound of ethereal music → **p. 39**

● *A sunny day at sea*
From the picture-postcard port of Kerýneia, the beautiful two-master *Barbarossa* heads for the beaches along the northern coast on a daily basis. Step aboard, allow the coast to drift past and soak up the sun on deck → **p. 95**

● *Feel good with feng shui*
In the environmentally-friendly *Hotel E* at Perivólia near Lárnaka you can take advantage of the feng shui feelgood factor that conditioned the layout of the building. The cherry on the relaxation cake is the fabulous Mediterranean gourmet cuisine served in the hotel's own restaurant → **p. 42**

● *Seaside hermitage*
If a light ocean breeze and the view from your bed through the open door onto the sea, only two paces away, are creature comfort enough for you, then the holiday cottages offered by the *Oasis at Ayfilon* taverna near Dipkarpaz/Rizokárpaso – not dissimilar to monk's cells – will be a true paradise for you → **p. 90**

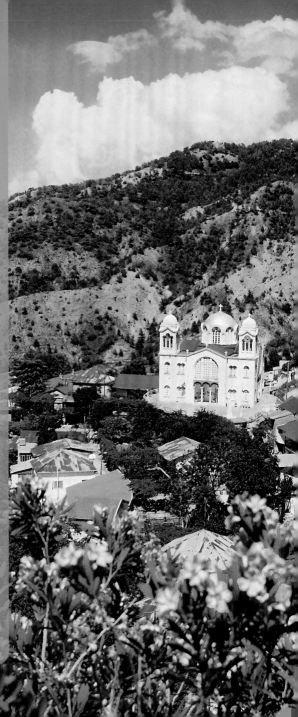

INTRODUCTION

DISCOVER CYPRUS!

Aphrodite, the beautiful goddess of love, is said to have been a Cyprus girl. This sunny island in the furthest east of the Mediterranean is truly an adequate home for a beauty expert, with its long dream beaches, crystal-clear waters, and wild and dramatic coasts. Two striking mountain ranges define the landscape; Gothic cathedrals, Turkish mosques, Byzantine monasteries and crusaders' castles characterise its culture. If it wasn't for this big ugly scar cutting right through the island and right through its vibrant capital ... a border drawn up by force in 1974. While the border is omnipresent in Cypriots' minds and emotions, as a foreign visitor you'll hardly be aware of it, allowing you to spend a relaxing Mediterranean holiday as peaceful as anywhere else.

Coming from the southern coastal resorts to the island metropolis of Nicosia, travellers will nearly invariably get off the bus at the nearly 500 year-old city wall or park their hire car in the wall ditch, or might stay night in a hotel on the 4km (2½mi)-long wall surrounding the entire Old Town. The city hall, dating from British colonial

Photo: View of Pedoulas village in the Tróodos mountain range

Visitor magnet in the Turkish part of the capital: the large caravanserai of Büyük Han

days, can be found on one of its bastions and is flanked by the colourful flags of countries in the EU that Cyprus has also been a part of since 2004. From there, Lidras Street leads as a straight-as-a-die pedestrian street into the middle of the Old Town.

> **Cross-border traffic is part of everyday life**

Small modern shops present enticing displays of shoes, clothes and jewellery; street cafés, restaurants and ice cream parlours are always busy. At one of the street corners a bingo player has been inviting passers-by to a game every evening for decades. All of this reflects everyday Cypriot life. But after 600 m the normality stops. This is where visitors pass a Greek-Cypriot border post, to walk a few yards through the buffer zone controlled by UN soldiers. On the other,

7000–1050 BC
Cyprus is settled by people from mainland Asia Minor

1050–294 BC
Era of the city kingdoms

294 BC–391 AD
Cyprus becomes a province of the Egyptian Ptolemean Empire, becoming Roman from 58 BC onwards

391–1191
Cyprus belongs to the Eastern Roman Empire, later to the Byzantine Empire

1191–1489
Cyprus is governed by Frankish kings

1489–1571
The island belongs to Venice

the Turkish-Cypriot side, they'll have to show their passports and fill in an immigration form. After that, everything is normal again, the historical buildings as pretty as in the southern part. And yet, a bit different – the locals here are Muslims instead of Christians, speak Turkish instead of Greek, have a different passport and a different government. Yet the people here also like to sit in street cafés and throw dice in the same board game, which some call *távli,* others *tavla.* Different, yet the same.

In the three large cities on the southern coast – Limassol, Lárnaka and Páfos – you won't feel the division. They seem modern and well-looked after. English is spoken in nearly all the hotels, restaurants and shops. Menus and signposts are bilingual. The coasts of Cyprus are varied: miles of sandy beaches fringe nearly the entire eastern coast north of Famagusta and the southern coast at Lárnaka; there are sandy coves at Agía Nápa and west of Páfos, near Limassol and also in the north near Kerýneia. Pebble beaches line the coast at Pólis.

Every part of Cyprus has its own mountain range. At 1026m (3366ft) high, up to 6km (3½mi) wide and 100km (62mi) long, the Kerýneia mountain range in the northern part borders

Monasteries and crusader castles

the coast looking towards Anatolia. With its bizarre needlepoint peaks, dramatic rock faces and striking rocky knolls, the landscape appears alpine, while the Tróodos mountain range in the south despite its 1951m (6400ft)-high Mount Olympus and

1571–1878
Cyprus becomes part of the Ottoman Empire, with many Turks settling on the island

1878–1925
Great Britain leases Cyprus from the Ottoman Empire for its strategic position

1925
The island becomes a British crown colony

1960
Cyprus gains independence, with archbishop Makários III as president

1963/64
Civil war starts; the first UN peacekeeping forces arrive in Cyprus

a circumference of 60km (37mi) looks more like a low, green mountain range. In the many valleys of the Tróodos range fruit and nut trees thrive; wine is grown up to altitudes of over 1000m (3280ft). While three crusaders' fortresses attract visitors to the Kerýneia range, the Tróodos mountains are brimful with monasteries and barn-roofed churches – so called for shape of their tiled roofs, typical for Cyprus. Over 20 of them still boast medieval wall paintings, with many of them listed as Unesco World Heritage sites.

Driving through the mountain valleys you'll come across abandoned villages again and again where Turkish Cypriots used to live up until 1974. After the Turkish invasion in July 1974 and the subsequent division of the island, they left the area. Lasting one month, the war had its origin in the putsch against president Makários III, instigated by the Greek military dictatorship with a view to annexing Cyprus to Greece. The Turks intervened in order to prevent this from happening. In the wake of the war over 150,000 Greek Cypriots fled from the Turkish-occupied north to the south, while over 45,000 Turkish Cypriots left the south to settle in the north.

> **Relaxed serenity is what Cypriots value most in life**

A small café in the Tróodos village of *Kakopetriá* – listed in its entirety by the way – is called 'I Galíni', roughly translatable as 'pleasant serenity'. Sitting here at one of the tiny tables on the small terrace under shady broadleaf trees above the roaring brook and sipping a small Cypriot coffee conveys precisely that feeling so important to many Cypriots as something to aspire to. As a traveller you'll also experience it when you mingle with the visitors market in the cafés in front of the market hall in Limassol's Old Town or go for an evening stroll between palm trees, beach and street cafés along the sea promenade of Lárnaka.

Serene are even the feral donkeys that will probably try and bump into your car on the Karpaz peninsula in the far northeast. These donkeys are amongst the few larger animals that have defied the modern urban sprawl on an island that has not exactly excelled in environmental awareness. Locked in a fight for survival however are the large sea turtles heading in large numbers for Golden Beach as well as Lára Beach west of Páfos in the summer in particular, to lay their eggs.

1974
Turkish invasion of Cyprus following a putsch against Makários staged by the Greek military junta; the island is divided

1977
Death of Makários

1983
Unilateral proclamation of the 'Turkish Republic of Northern Cyprus'

2004
In April 75.8 % of southern Cypriots vote against re-unification. On 1 May only southern Cyprus becomes a member of the EU

2008
The euro becomes the national currency

Beast of burden? Not here: the feral donkeys of the northeast are free to enjoy life

Sometimes the beaches line tiny bays such as Fig Tree Bay or Kónnos Bay in Protarás, often they extend along the coast for miles and open up as wide as a football field with fine sand or colourful pebbles. Paragliders sail through the air dangling from their parachutes, divers descend to sea caves and shipwrecks. Cyprus is a great place for sports, offering a good variety on dry land too, with signposted hiking trails and mountain bike 'stations', several golf courses and

What Aphrodite appreciated most on her island were the quiet hidden corners

a number of riding stables. At night the dancing fever knows no bounds: Agía Nápa is considered the clubbing mecca of the eastern Mediterranean, while in Limassol in particular you can experience first hand how the locals party in music clubs and traditional taverns.

Aphrodite though appreciated more the quiet, calm places of her home island of Cyprus. Far from the beach of Pétra tou Romíou, where she rose from the waters for the first time, and Páfos, the location of her most important sanctuary, she met her lover Akamás in a small spring pool at what is today Pólis to spend hours tenderly caressing right by the sea. To sit here on a restaurant terrace, enjoying fresh fish and a glass of Cypriot wine, looking out over the wide bay at the sea, gently aware of the light carob tree groves on the slopes around you, transports even the most stressed holidaymaker into the calm world that Cypriots aspire to – pleasant serenity.

WHAT'S HOT

1 Performance

Art The *Pantheon Urban Soul Festival* in Nicosia unites many art forms: dance and theatre, object and performance art *(Trípoli Park, www.pantheonculture.org, photo)*. One of the acts taking part in the festival every year is the *DrumInspire* percussion group *(Voróklini, www.druminspire.com)*, as well as the *Echo Arts Center* run by Ariánna Económou. The artist, the owner of a dance theatre, holds modern dance workshops *(Vasileos Pavlou 67b, Kaimakli, Nicosia, www.echo-arts.info)*.

In harmony

2

Natural well-being The spa establishments on Cyprus have taken nature as their guide. At the *Agíi Anárgýri Spa* everything is perfect down to the last detail, including the surroundings – the modern resort is in a former monastery *(Páfos, www.ayiian argyrisparesort.com)*. The spa at *Le Meridien* boasts the largest thalasso therapy basin in Europe *(Nicosia Road, Limassol, photo)*. Cyprus even has its own organic line of cosmetics: *Neoderma* produces high-quality creams and lotions without genetical engineering or animal testing *(www.neoderma.com)*.

Herbal task force

3

Aromatic little helpers Ever browsed a herbal library? Expand your knowledge on herbs with the *CyHerbia Nature Project*, and put it into practice in the herbal garden *(Avgorou, www. cyprushealingherbs.com)*. The workshops run by *Earth Herbals* will teach you how to make your own creams, oils and teas from herbs *(Akamás, www.heavenonearthherbals.com)*. The *Sienna Restaurant* provides a gourmet experience in the herbal garden. Oregano, basil and coriander all contribute to that Cypriot flavour *(Chlorakas Avenue, Páfos, photo)*.

Downhill & cross-country

Going down Cyprus is a classic dream destination for cyclists and, slowly, a downhill and cross-country cycling scene is developing here now. If you're not afraid of steep gradients, get on your bike to Voróklini, the starting point for an artificial downhill run, at over 200m (650ft) above sea level. This is also where the *Oroklini Downhill Race* takes place, where Andreas Pettemerides of *Limassol Sporting Club* has regularly been crowned champion *(http://limassol sportingclub.terapad.com)*. The recent downhill scene is supported by *Fenistal*, the representative for *Bergamont Bicycles* with a test centre in Nicosia *(Tseriou Avenue 150, www.bergamont.de, site also in English)*. If you'd rather bike cross-country than downhill you will feel more at home with the island's Cross-country community which meets at least once a year for the *Sunshine Cup* *(www.cyclingcy.com, photo)*.

Agritourism

Getting away from it all It's not just the gorgeous resorts that the Cypriots love, but the old stone cottages. To preserve them, many little cottages have been equipped with modern cons. There are also very comfortable villas for rent, such as in the small village of Tochní *(www.tochni villas.com)* which has perfected agritourism, as well as in Buyukkonuk on the Turkish side of the island. Here you can soak up village life, collect olives to be pressed the old way, bake bread, look after goats or make your own Halloumi cheese *(www.eco tourismcyprus.com, photo)*. Through renting out the stone cottages, the *Leona Foundation* is also contributing to the preservation of the traditional way of life *(www.conservation.org.cy)*.

IN A NUTSHELL

BEACHES

In southern Cyprus all beaches apart from the organised lidos set up by the tourist authorities are free of charge, while on the northern coast around Kerýneia a few beaches are leased to private owners who charge. All popular beaches rent out deckchairs and sunshades and, in summer, there is usually a lifeguard on duty.

BIRDHUNTING

Nearly entirely unknown to the general public and tourists, over a thousand bird-hunters still ply their murderous trade; there are no figures for northern Cyprus. As some Cypriots are mad about eating songbirds, they achieve high black market prices which has led to the devel-

opment of more or less mafia-style structures amongst hunters. The trade of the chirpy little birds caught with nets and lime branches is solely conducted under the counter.

BYZANTIUM

On Cyprus you can't step out without treading on something Byzantine. For Cyprus, Byzantium forms the connection with Greece, which has been casting itself in the role of its successor since the foundation of the state of modern Greece in 1830, and even more so since the demise of Tsarist Russia. While Cyprus has never formed part of Greece, it was a part of Byzantium together with Greece: in 330, Emperor Constantine moved the capital of the Roman Empire to the

Whether Byzantium or the EU, history has left its traces in stone – and is one of the reasons behind the political problems still confronting Cyprus

shores of the Bosporus. In 395, when Emperor Theodosius divided the Roman Empire, the city, now named Constantinople, became the centre of the Eastern Roman Empire that we call Byzantium. When the Turks conquered Byzantium in 1453, they named it Istanbul.

FAUNA

The wildlife of Cyprus has suffered from the enormous urban sprawl. The one particularly conspicuous species are the many thousand pink flamingos

perching in the saline lakes of Lárnaka and Akrotíri in winter, the countless swifts and house-martins, as well as the *hardun*, a lizard that seems to have come right out of prehistory and measures up to 30cm. A heavily endangered species are the marine turtles *Caretta caretta*, who lay their eggs on the island's sandy beaches in the peak of summer, the griffon vultures circling the skies in parts of the remote mountains, and the eight types of snake living on Cyprus, of which only three are poisonous. The shy wild mouflon sheep, still numbering some 2000 that hide themselves away in the western part of Tróodos, is considered the national animal.

FLEET

Would you believe it: small Cyprus counts amongst the ten biggest seafaring nations in the world, occupying third place even within the EU. Just over 1000 ships, with an overall tonnage of 20.2 million sail under the Cypriot flag of convenience. What the mostly foreign ship owners appreciate about Cyprus is the low level of bureaucracy and the low taxes – as well as the lower rates of pay for the seamen.

FLORA

Cyprus is a particularly densely forested Mediterranean island. Today, a fifth of its surface is again covered in trees, after thousands of years of logging for ship and house building, as well as for fuel. The coastal regions are dominated by olive and carob trees, the beaches feature mostly tamarisks and the rural roads are lined with eucalyptus trees, while cypresses and acacia provide some variety. The higher-altitude regions have thriving Aleppo pines, evergreen oaks, poplars, nut and fruit trees, as well as over 30,000 cedar trees in the west of the Tróodos mountain range. The summit regions feature juniper and black

Agricultural livestock benefitting from agricultural crops: sheep seeking shade under olive trees

pines. All in all, Cyprus has about 1800 types of plants, of which over 120 are endemic, only occurring in the wild on this island. The island's most important cultivated plant is vine. Cereals grow mainly on the Mesaória, the plain between the island's two mountain ranges. Citrus fruit are grown on a large scale on the northern coast and in the plantations of Fasoúri west of Limassol, potatoes near Agía Nápa and bananas as well as peanuts around Páfos. In the spring, Cyprus is a sea of flowers. Particularly conspicuous are the asphodels and rockroses, hyacinths and narcissi, cyclamen and peonies, poppies, oleander and gorse, as well as hibiscus and bougainvillea as ornamental plants.

No getting away from it: UN sentry box on the Green Line

FOREIGNERS

Over the past 800 years, the fate of Cyprus has been determined by foreigners. Since 1191 the island has been governed by outside dynasties speaking a different language and professing different beliefs if not of an entirely different religion. The first ones to arrive were the Roman Catholic crusaders, followed by the Venetians, later the Turks and, last but not least, the English. Great Britain, Greece and Turkey drew up the constitution for the modern state of Cyprus without involving a single Cypriot. Since 1964 UN soldiers from all over the world have been stationed on the island – while in 1974 Turkish troops also returned. They were followed by staff working for international firms, enticed by numerous tax concessions in southern Cyprus. After the collapse of the Soviet Union, many Russians came to invest their dubious monies on the island in companies and then legally transfered those monies back to the CIS states – today, some 20,000 Russian companies operate in southern Cyprus, most of them no more than a mail-

ing address; 40,000 Russians live here. A fair number of British citizens live on the island too; many of them have a second house in the north or in the south – and about 20,000 are stationed on the two large military bases in southern Cyprus that Great Britain was able to secure for itself during the 1959/60 independence negotiations – for all time and without paying anything for the lease. All this makes the 2.5 million tourists coming to Cyprus every year a near-negligible quantity of temporary guests.

GREEN LINE

Cyprus has been divided since 1974. A 215km (134mi)-long demarcation line cuts off the north, predominantly settled by Turkish Cypriots, from the south, inhabited by an overwhelming majority of Greek Cypriots. Nicosia's Old Town was divided as early as 1964, the division line being marked with a green felt-tip pen on a map of the city, earning it the name Green Line, which is now being used for the entire demarcation line.

As a tourist outside Nicosia you'll only be aware of the course the Green Line takes due to the watchtowers and flags. It represents no danger to tourists. In Nicosia itself, the Green Line is marked by a simple low wall, fortified by blue-and-white painted oil barrels and sandbags. In parts it actually follows the medieval city wall.

CONS

Representations of saints and biblical events on panels are known in the Orthodox church as icons. You'll find them in all churches and many private homes, on the dashboard of overland buses and in the wheelhouses of fishing boats. Icons are completely different from the images of Christian-religious content in our churches. Rather than being a decorative object, they bring the saint into the house, making him real and present. Being considered 'gateways to heaven', they enjoy particular veneration, are kissed and adorned with gold, silver, precious stones and wrapped in sumptuously embroidered material. Icons are consulates of heaven on earth and are treated as if they were the saints themselves.

RRIGATION

Like many Mediterranean islands, Cyprus too suffered from a lack of water for a long time. With the 1990s the problem has been more or less solved. The extensive precipitation of the winter months is captured by over 100 dammed lakes and reservoirs in the Tróodos mountain range and channelled via canals and pipelines to the big towns and the fields in the plains. Additional relief is provided by two seawater desalination plants in the south. In particularly dry years however drinking water still has to be imported by boat from Greece.

Always decked out beautifully: icons

This unnatural border is still being watched over by soldiers from three parties. In the north, Turkish and Turkish-Cypriot units stand at the ready, in the south Greek and Greek-Cypriot. The strip of land between them, between 10m and over 40m wide, the so-called buffer zone, is patrolled by soldiers of the *UN-FICYP* United Nations peace troops in order to prevent a direct confrontation between the parties and to be able to solve any problems at the lowest-possible level.

MAKÁRIOS III

Holidaymakers still meet the archbishop who reigned in the first 17 years of independence on many photographs and in the shape of massive monuments. For most southern Cypriots, he is the father figure, whose politics are practically above criticism. Born in 1913 as the son of peasants in the mountain village of Páno Panagiá in Tróodos, the 11-year old entered Kýkko Monastery and later studied theology. In 1948 he was elected bishop of Kition (Lárnaka), and just 2½ years later he became the archbishop of the island.

Makários also became the political leader of the Greek Cypriots, flanking the armed struggle against the colonial power with flaming speeches. It was practically inevitable that he should be elected the first president of the new republic in 1960 – holding on to his job as primate of the church at the same time. In the years that followed, Makários tried to push back the strong influence the constitution allowed the Turkish Cypriots in administration, politics and the police. The military measures he allowed to be taken against Turkish Cypriots fanned the flames of tension.

In terms of foreign policy Makários fought for the non-alignment of Cyprus and for less economic dependency on Britain. When in 1967 the military took power in Greece, president Makários moved away from his attempts to achieve *énosis,* the return under the wing of Greece, condemning the dictatorship of the colonels in Athens. In 1974, the military engineered his overthrow. After the Turkish invasion Makários returned to Cyprus, where he stayed up to his death in 1977, his powers limited however to presiding over the division of his country.

RELIGION

Nearly all Greek Cypriots profess to belonging to the Greek Orthodox Catholic church which allows its priests to marry before taking the sacraments. The Orthodox church does not accept the Pope's authority as head of the church. Baptism is by full immersion and the first communion is received straight after christening. There are further differences in the field of dogma. Nearly all Turkish Cypriots are Sunni Muslims. Few of them are strictly observant; the ban on alcohol and the fasting rules in the month of Ramadan are rarely observed. A much more conservative attitude with regards to Islam has been brought to northern Cyprus from 1974 onwards by the many new settlers from rural areas of Anatolia.

YOUTH

Cypriot's youth seems to enjoy life. During the day, cafés and bars are full of well-dressed young people, who at weekends in summer crowd the beaches and clubs. Nearly everybody has a mobile phone, often also a car or motorbike. However, while public protests are rare, below the surface things aren't all that calm. The general prosperity of the past 20 years and the foundation of universities on Cyprus itself have led to more and more pupils taking A-levels and going on to study in their home country or abroad. Jobs for graduates however are thin on the ground. Many young people are forced to emigrate. Those who stay often remain living at home until they get married, to save money. Nor is it easy to find jobs to improve finances, as a large foreign workforce from all over the world stands at the ready to fill vacancies for the minimum wage guaranteed by the state.

FOOD & DRINK

The food on Cyprus is the result of many foreign influences. Turkish, Oriental, Italian, Asian and British components ensure variety and the use of interesting spices.

The Cypriots prefer to use home-grown produce and prepare dishes in the clay oven or on the charcoal grill to using the hob. Meat is consumed in great quantities as fish is too expensive. Pulses are popular, while caper twigs and coriander leaves are often added to salads. A lot of vegetables are also eaten raw or pickled. It's actually not difficult to get to know a large number of Cypriot specialities in a single evening. Nearly all restaurants praise their *mesé* (pronounced 'meh-zeh'), consisting of between 12 and 20 different dishes served on small plates, with everybody helping themselves to how much they like. You have the choice between meat, fish and sometimes purely vegetarian *mesé*.

DRINKS

On Cyprus good food is always accompanied by a good wine. Up until recently wine was the island's most important export article. There's a wide range available which now also includes organic wines. Northern Cyprus doesn't have much of a winegrowing industry, preferring to drink wine imported from Turkey. Beer is brewed on Cyprus too. Breweries in southern Cyprus produce the *Keó* and *Carlsberg* brands. In the north, the beer of choice is the Turkish *Efes* or the

Photo: Cypriot starters

**Refreshing Brandy Sour:
the Cypriot national drink is a reminder
of colonial days**

Goldfässl brand brewed under Austrian licence.

For a home-grown aperitif choose between sherry and ouzo. Recommended digestifs are the bitter orange liqueur *filfar*, the *commandaría* dessert wine and Cypriot brandy. *Five Kings* is considered the best brand of brandy. *Brandy Sour*, the refreshing long drink mixed from brandy, lemon or lime syrup and soda water, is a reminder of the time the English spent here and has become the Cypriot national drink. The non-alcoholic

speciality of northern Cyprus is *ayran*, a mixture of water and yoghurt with some salt and dried peppermint. Surprisingly, freshly squeezed juice is rarely on offer and given the number of orange and fruit plantations it is just far too expensive.

EATING OUT

Going out to eat somewhere else that in your hotel will take you on a culinary trip around the world. There is a wide range

LOCAL SPECIALITIES

▶ **afélia** – marinated pork, braised in red wine and fairly fatty

▶ **chiroméri** – salted goat meat

▶ **choriatikí saláta** – farmer's salad with feta cheese and olives (photo)

▶ **dolmádes** – vine leaves stuffed with rice and sometimes mincemeat

▶ **hallúmi** – halloumi, Cypriot cheese made with sheep's and goat's milk, usually eaten grilled

▶ **humús** – a puree made of chickpeas, olive oil, parsley and garlic

▶ **kléftiko** – Cypriot national dish. Baked lamb or goat meat with potatoes, prepared if you're lucky in the traditional clay oven (oftón)

▶ **kúpes/kupékia** – doughballs made of coarsely ground wheat, stuffed with pork mince, onions and parsley

▶ **lachanodolmádes** – small cabbage roulades, stuffed with rice and mince and served warm

▶ **lúndsa** – a kind of smoked pork chop, usually served in thin slices

▶ **paidákia** – lamb cutlets

▶ **ravióles** – large ravioli filled with cheese and often a pinch of mint too

▶ **scheftaliá** – well seasoned grilled sausages made of pork mince in a lamb's stomach lining

▶ **stifádo** – pork, beef or rabbit goulash in a tomato sauce seasoned with cinnamon or cumin

▶ **supjés** – a type of octopus usually served whole or stuffed, always fresh from the sea, in contrast to the better-known kalamáres from the deep freezer

▶ **súvla** – grill skewer with nearly fist-sized pieces of meat

▶ **suvláki** – the smaller variation with fork-sized pieces of meat

▶ **tachíni** – a thick sauce made of sesame, olive oil, garlic, lemon juice, especially popular as a starter

▶ **talatúri** – a sauce similar to Greek tzatziki, made with yoghurt, cucumber, olive oil and garlic (photo)

▶ **taramosaláta** – reddish puree made of fish roe and mashed potato

of Italian, Asian, French and Lebanese-Syrian restaurants, while the Polynesian, Russian, Spanish and Latin American cuisines are also well represented. Gýros, doner kebab, pizza, toasted sandwiches and burgers round off the choice. Menus are nearly always bilingual (Greek or Turkish and English). Bread is always served with your food and it'll appear on the bill even if you've not eaten any of it. Most restaurants are open from noon–3pm and between 7pm–11pm. Reservations are only really necessary for larger groups or top restaurants.

HOTEL FOOD

Standards at Cypriot hotel restaurants are high. Breakfast reveals the British influence. In the higher-class hotels, sausages, rashers and eggs or omelettes feature on the breakfast buffet, in the more basic establishments you can order them for an additional charge.

At lunch and dinnertime there are often Cypriot dishes on offer too. Many establishments set up a dinner buffet once or twice a week, which allows you to try a good number of Cypriot specialities, *mesé*-style.

COFFEESHOPS & PASTRY SHOPS

Bakery/pastry shops are only found in the towns. Their Greek name is *sacharoplastío,* their Turkish name *pastahane* and they serve drinks (though no wine) as well as sweets and Oriental cakes. On Cyprus, sweet things also include a variety of fruit and vegetables marinated in sugar syrup, such as cherry tomatoes, walnuts harvested while unripe, bergamot oranges, cherries, plums, aubergines and grapes. The collective noun for all these treats served on a small plate with a teaspoon and cake fork is *gliká tou koutoulioú.*

Everywhere in the towns and in nearly every village you'll find coffeehouses, called *kafeníon* (Turkish *kahvehani*) in the singular. Tables with felt tops are used to play cards, draughts and *távli* (backgammon). Beverages on sale include softdrinks, beer and coffee or tea, in southern Cyprus also *tsiwanía* (distilled fermented vine stems and grape skins similar to grappa), ouzo or brandy – and last, but definitely not least, whisky. Instant coffee is available and always called *Nescafé*; it is also consumed cold, frappé-style. The standard drink on Cyprus however is mocha, which you order as *kafé*, indicating how you'd like it to be made: *skétto* (Turkish *sadez)* – without sugar; *métrio* (Turkish *ortai)* – with a little sugar; *warígliko* (Turkish *sekerli)* – with a lot of sugar.

Cypriot way of life: al fresco eating and drinking

SHOPPING

Cyprus is not exactly shopper's heaven. The range of original souvenirs is fairly limited.

ANTIQUES

If you love the patina of age, go browsing the antique shops of Nicosia's Old Town that sell not only tables, beds and cupboards, but also objects that are easier to take home: porcelain, watches, jewellery, cutlery and glass from the British colonial era in particular.

CRAFTS

Small woven rugs and colourful embroidery work can be found in many places. Pottery is produced in both parts of Cyprus in great quantities. Several potteries line the old coastal road heading east out of Geroskípou. Pretty baskets are made in Geroskípou and Liopétri. You can get them at a particularly good price in the market halls of these towns. The oblong baskets used by bird catchers to carry their lime branches make an original umbrella stand. Wooden chairs with braided seats can be ordered from craftsmen in the mountain village of Phíni.

CULINARY ITEMS

On your hunt for souvenirs don't forget the island's culinary specialities: Cypriot sherry, ouzo or brandy, *filfar* or *commandaría* are not easily available at home outside London or other cities with a large Cypriot community. Thyme honey, marinated fruit, *hallúmi* sheep's cheese or *lukúmia* (similar to jelly fruit) from Geroskípou and Páno Léfkara back home will help revive that holiday feeling. Cypriot peanuts and pecan nuts, best bought at the markets or stalls in the Tróodos mountains also make tasty little gifts. This is where you can buy jars of fruit soaked in sugar syrup such as bergamots, quinces and walnuts harvested green and blackened in the jar. Make sure the lids of the jars are really tight and the jars not sticky!

FASHION

Cypriot designers who went on to a career abroad include Sía Dimitriádi, Joánna Loúca, Ioánna Kourbéla, Élena Pávlou and Dóra Schabel. Their designs for women's fashions can be found in a number of good boutiques on the island.

Hallúmi cheese, icons and the art of the hemstitch: when buying souvenirs, go for quality and Cypriot crafts

FOLK ART

Folk art products are popular souvenirs. Hemstitch embroidery has been produced for centuries in the village of Páno Léfkara. It adorns tablecloths, napkins, blouses and handkerchiefs. Authentic lefkarítika has its price – the cheap copies sold in Páno Léfkara were made in Asia. Filigree silver work is produced in Páno Léfkara, too, as well as in other places.

ICONS

Hand-painted icons make a special souvenir. The best place to buy them is direct from icon painters, e.g. in Limassol, Ómodos or at Ágios Minás Monastery.

LEATHER GOODS

Shoes, leather goods and textiles produced on Cyprus itself are attractively priced. Buyers should however have some idea of what they're looking for and be able to judge the quality, as there is any amount of low-quality cheap and cheerful produce. Comparing the price for similar goods, the north is often cheaper than the south. Limassol's Old Town also has several specialist shops that make shoes made to measure. Tailors for menswear offer their made-to-measure services in all towns in southern Cyprus.

MUSEUM REPLICAS

Cyprus hasn't yet discovered the sales potential of certified replicas of beautiful museum objects. A few specimens can be found in the museum shop of the Cyprus Museum in Nicosia or in the Pierides Collection in Lárnaka. The best selection is at the *Triskélion Pottery* in the village of Neo Chorió near Pólis *(Mon–Fri 10.30am–5pm, Sat 10am–1pm | www. triskelionpottery.com)*.

THE PERFECT ROUTE

FROM THE BEACH TO THE DIVIDED CAPITAL

After a relaxing day at the beach and in the Old Town of ① *Lárnaka* → p. 37 take the service taxi to your hotel in the divided island capital, ② *Nicosia* → p. 52 with its many museums, historical monuments and fine taverns.

IN THE TURKISH NORTH OF THE ISLAND

Walk along the Old Town's main thoroughfare, Lídra Street, across the border into the Turkish-Cypriot part and take a taxi to ③ *Girne/Kerýneia* → p. 93. Take a leisurely stroll through the Old Town, enjoy the harbour, lined by fish taverns and cafés and book a hire car for the next two days. Drive up to the medieval ④ *St Hilárion Castle* → p. 97 and the Gothic ⑤ *Bellapaís Monastery* → p. 95 (photo left). The next day take a long drive through the alpine Kerýneia mountains to the once famously wealthy city of ⑥ *Famagusta* → p. 87 and the extensive excavations of ⑦ *Sálamis* → p. 92, which is a great place for a dip too.

NIGHT IN NICOSIA

After a further night in Kerýneia, take a taxi back to the checkpoint in ② *Nicosia* → p. 52 or straight to your hotel there and spend another night on the Greek-Cypriot side of the capital. Now you can shop to your heart's content, as the next morning you're picking up your hire car for the entire second part of your trip.

CHURCHES AND MONASTERIES IN THE TRÓODOS MOUNTAINS

A first exploration of the foothills of the Tróodos mountains leads you to the barn-roofed church of ⑧ *Asinoú* → p. 61, gloriously painted inside and boasting Unesco World Heritage status. Afterwards drive through lonely mountainous countryside to the famous ⑨ *Kýkko Monastery* → p. 80. Spend the night nearby in ⑩ *Pedoulás* → p. 82, a quiet and very typical mountain village. Drive on bendy roads untouched by mass tourism through dense forests to the northern coast, where your destination now is the easy-going small town of ⑪ *Pólis* → p. 74 with many fine beaches (photo right).

Discover the many facets of Cyprus from north to south, through the divided capital and two magnificent mountain ranges

ON THE TRAIL OF APHRODITE

It's a good idea to spend two nights at ⑫ *Páfos* → p. 64 with its many sights, before heading off again via ⑬ *Koúklia* → p. 73 with its Aphrodite sanctuary and the Rocks of Aphrodite to ⑭ *Pissoúri* → p. 51, where you can choose between the mountain village or a beach cottage for your accommodation.

ANTIQUITY FIRST, MOUNTAINS LATER

Visiting the extensive excavations of ⑮ *Koúrion* → p. 50 requires half a day, leaving you enough time in the afternoon to take a look at the city of ⑯ *Limassol* → p. 44 right by the sea and to enjoy its rich nightlife. The next day, a detour leads you once again up into the Tróodos mountains. Your destinations here are ⑰ *Ómodos* → p. 82 with its idyllic monastery and one of the most beautiful village squares in the country, as well as cityfolk's summer retreat from the heat, ⑱ *Páno Plátres* → p. 82 nestling just below the Cypriot Mount Olympus.

SHOPPING

The drive back to Lárnaka leads you to the excavations of ⑲ *Choirokoitía* → p. 41 and far back into Cypriot history. Afterwards feel free to devote yourself to shopping for souvenirs in the photogenic mountain village of ⑳ *Páno Léfkara* → p. 42 and to reward yourself enjoying the beautify of the Cypriot landscape.

800km (approx. 500mi).
Driving time: 16 hours.
Recommended time: 2 weeks.
Detailed map of the route in the road atlas, the pull-out map and on the back cover

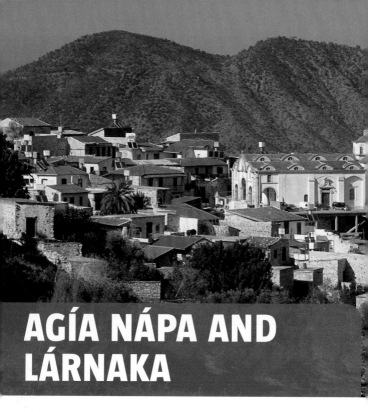

AGÍA NÁPA AND LÁRNAKA

Finally: the beach! Nowhere else in southern Cyprus will you find strips of sand longer and wider than at Agía Nápa and Paralímni-Protarás in the far southeast of the island. The water in shallow Níssi Bay shimmers in all imaginable shades of blue and turquoise, and at the beach due east from the busy boat harbour of Agía Nápa the wind has formed low dunes.

Everything in this region of Cyprus is geared towards holidays – the up-to-date resorts have relegated agriculture to the hinterland. The region is flat and ideal for cycle tours, while good-value buses regularly connect the coastal towns with each other. Boats ply the coastline, hiking trails are well marked and the watersports on offer here range from paragliding to wreck diving. If you want to concentrate on a beach holiday, Agía Nápa and Paralímni-Protarás will look after you very well – however, you'll be furthest away from all the sights of the island.

In Lárnaka you'll dive into the life of the locals. The wide city beach stretches out right in front of the busy Old Town, motorways take you in under an hour to the two largest cities of the island, Nicosia and Limassol. In simple coffeehouses you'll sit among Cypriot pensioners and businessmen, while the chic bars of the waterfront promenade provide you with a front seat for watching the evening entertainment provided by the Cypriot youth.

Photo: Village view of Páno Léfkara

Between beaches and hills: tourism sets the pace in the major coastal resorts while the rest of the region is still largely agricultural

AGÍA NÁPA

(139 E4) (*ℳ L–M7*) **Agía Nápa (pop. 2500) is a coastal town thought up on the drawing board which shows its youth everywhere you go. Still, the planners have managed to avoid marring the landscape with unsuitable or bombastic buildings.**

The only thing that's old about Agía Nápa is the medieval monastery that formed the nucleus around which the new town centre grew up. You'll find a true picture-postcard idyll at the fishing port. Between mid-April and end of October Agía Nápa attracts mainly younger holidaymakers who appreciate the intense nightlife of the town as much as the pretty beaches and the many opportunities for water sports. In the wintertime only those looking for peace and quiet will enjoy themselves: most clubs and bars are closed then; in the colder season many restaurants only open at the weekend.

Only the monastery in Agía Napa with its pretty fountain is old

particular charm from its location right on the sea. *Openly accessible*

AGÍA NÁPA MONASTERY

From the secluded inner courtyard of the monastery, founded around 1530 with its fountain house and ancient gargoyle in the shape of a boar's head, steps lead down into the cave church of the monastery. The mulberry tree standing in front of the monastery's southern gate is over 400 years old. *In the centre, on the main street leading to the fishing port | openly accessible*

THÁLASSA

The main attraction of this modern maritime museum is the seaworthy replica of a sailing freighter which sank 2300 years ago off the coast of Kerýneia. On view is also a papyrus boat of a type that was still used on Greek islands in the early years of the last century. *June–Sept Sun 9am–1pm, Mon–Sat 9am–1pm and 6–10pm, Oct–May Mon 9am–1pm, Tue–Sat 9am–5pm | admission 3 euros | Krío Neró Avenue 14*

FOOD & DRINK

ESPERIA ☆

Classy tavern with a large terrace on the fishing port; pretty view of Cape Gréko. Good selection of dishes, also of fresh fish. *Daily from noon | Archiepieskopou Makariou III 46 | Expensive*

INSIDER TIP NÁPA ●

One of the first tavernas established in the town back in 1976. Large selection of Cypriot specialities. Vegetarians also catered for too. Here, the walls replace the guestbook: generations of satisfied customers have left their (re)marks. *Daily from 4pm | Odós Dimokratías 15 | above the monastery | Moderate*

SIGHTSEEING

HELLENISTIC GRAVES

On the Makrónissos peninsula west of the centre, 19 graves were hewn into the rock in Hellenistic-Roman times. Steps lead down to the burial chambers where the deceased were buried in earthenware coffins. Even for those not overly keen on archaeology, this site gains its

SPORTS & BEACHES

Agía Nápa doesn't have the monopoly on beaches, there are more along the coast to the west, east and north of the town. They are easily accessible by bike, moped or hire car, and some beaches are served by pleasure boats. All larger beaches offer windsurfing, paragliding, waterskiing and pedal boats. Several diving schools operate here too.

ENTERTAINMENT

BED ROCK INN

This club is worth visiting even for those who hate discos, and even families, as this open-air bar is all about the Stone Age. Fred and Wilma Flintstone are everywhere, the barman wears a leopard skin and the DJ spins his tunes from the egg of a prehistoric bird. *Daily from 7pm | Odós Loúka Loúka | www.bedrockinn. com*

LUNA PARK

Fun park with merry-go-rounds for children, dodgems, big wheel, go-kart track, mini-golf, slingshot and trampoline. *Daily from noon | Níssi Avenue/corner of Makários III Avenue*

ROCK GARDEN

The owners of this open-air club like to call it 'The Official Mad House'. The playlist in the island's official asylum then consists of indie, alternative, classics and prog rock. *Daily from 6pm | Agías Mávris Street 2*

WHERE TO STAY

ELIGÓNIA

Spacious flats near the monastery, small pool in the tiny garden. Regulars appreciate the super central location near the nightlife district; many Scandinavians even spend the winter here. *22 rooms | Krío Neró Avenue 1 | tel. 23 81 92 92 | www. eligonia.com | Budget*

GRECIAN PARK

5-star hotel on a promontory between Cape Gréco national park and Protarás. Pool, indoor pool, beach on Kónnos Bay just over 300m below the hotel. Good walking options nearby and the beach boasts one of the best watersports outfits in Cyprus. *245 rooms | Kónnos Street 81 | tel. 23 83 20 00 | www.grecianpark. com | Expensive*

KÉRMIA BEACH

Bungalow complex in a very quiet location, 4km (2½mi) east of Agía Nápa, with a child-friendly beach. Large pool right on the beach, mountain bike hire. Good daytime bus connections into Agía Nápa and Protarás. *154 rooms | Kávo Gkreko Avenue 74 | tel. 23 72 14 01 | www.kermia hotels.com.cy | Expensive*

⭐ **Choirokoitía**
People were already living in this Stone Age village 8000 years ago → p. 41

⭐ **Halan Sultan Tekke**
Oriental flair on Lárnaka's salt lake → p. 41

⭐ **Panagía Angeloktístos**
Kíti boasts a mosaic not dissimilar to the famous one in Ravenna → p. 41

⭐ **Stavrovoúni Monastery**
Only men are allowed into the oldest monastery on Cyprus → p. 42

MARCO POLO HIGHLIGHTS

INFORMATION

CYPRUS TOURISM ORGANISATION
Krío Neró Avenue 12 | near the monastery | tel. 23 72 17 96

WHERE TO GO

AGÍA THÉKLA (139 E4) *(ℳ L7)*

Standing above the beach of the same name 7km (4½mi) west of Agía Nápa is the small modern *Chapel of Saint Thékla*. A white cross 10m away marks the entrance to an ancient *cave church* in a rock burial chamber from Hellenistic-Roman times. *Openly accessible*

DERÍNIA (DERÝNEIA) 🏖

(139 E3) *(ℳ L6)*

This large village, 10km (6½mi) northwest, nearly touches the demarcation line dividing northern Cyprus from the south. In the well-signed *Cultural Centre of Occupied Ammóchostos* you can watch English-language films on Famagusta and the Cyprus conflict seen from a Greek-Cypriot perspective. Use the binoculars provided to look across to Famagusta and the hotel town of *Varósha (Mon–Fri 7.30am–4.30pm, Sat 9.30am–4.30pm)*, which has been standing empty since 1974. Also worth seeing is the small *Derýneia Folk Museum* in the centre of town *(Mon–Sat open in daytime | admission 1.70 euros)*, showing the interior of a peasant's home before 1960. Good Cypriot food in old farmhouse surroundings can be found in *Taverna Fernági* in the town centre *(Mon–Sat from 6pm | Athinón Street 2 | Budget)*.

CAPE GRÉKO (AKROTÍRIO GKRÉKO)

(139 F4) *(ℳ M7)*

While the most southeasterly point of the island may not be visited due to the presence of military installations on the Cape, the 8km (5mi) drive there is very scenic. Along the way there are several options for detours to rocky coves and sandy beaches. The peninsula features six way-marked hiking trails; pick up the relevant brochures from the tourist information office.

NORTHERN CYPRUS

At the time of going to press, the nearest border checkpoint to northern Cyprus was at *Ágios Nikólaos* (139 D3) *(ℳ L5)* 3km (2mi) southwest of Famagusta. While this checkpoint is not served by buses, on the Greek-Cypriot side you can call a taxi on your return from the kafenío just beyond the British military checkpoint. And on the Turkish-Cypriot side it's easy to get a ride in a car. Bikes and hire cars don't present any problem when taken across.

PARALÍMNI-PROTARÁS

(139 E–F 3–4) *(ℳ L–M6)*

The hotel area in Protarás and *Pernéra* as well as a few more hotels further north belong to the large inland village of Paralímni, 5km (3mi) north of Agía, with three churches on the village square worth visiting. The modern *Café Senso (daily from 10am | Moderate)* on the edge of the square is a trendy meeting place for Cypriot hipsters. You'll find wraps and nachos as well as quality champagne costing up to 1000 euros a bottle!

Numerous sandy coves line the coast, many of them offering opportunities for water sports. For the most beautiful view across the region, head for the modern 🏖 *Profítis Ilías* chapel standing on a striking low rock on the western edge, coming from Protarás. Right next to the chapel you'll find four wishing trees. In the past, the faithful would knot kerchiefs into these trees to support their prayers. Today, tourists add trainers and bras.

Taverns, bars and clubs cluster along the pedestrianised Hotel Road in Protarás. This is also where you'll discover *Magic Dancing Waters,* presenting a grandiose water fountain show assisted by 18,000 jets, 480 floodlights and lots of music *(daily 9pm | admission 16 euros)*. Right on the bypass, on the crossroads at the traffic lights, at the height of the *Sfinx Bar* – unmissable thanks to its Egyptian decor – a surprise awaits: two small *galleries* with a unique INSIDER TIP collection of lead, silver and stainless steel objects made by South African designer Carrol Boyes *(www.carrol boyesshop.com)*, as well as china figures by the Spanish *Lladró* manufacture *(www. lladro.com)*.

INSIDER TIP PÓTAMOS TOU LIOPETRÍOU (139 E4) *(𝄜 L7)*

The river port, 12km (7½mi) west of Agía Nápa, is considered the most authentic fishing port in Cyprus. Hundreds of small boats are moored here. On the shore you can choose between two simple fish taverns.

LÁRNAKA

(138 B5) *(𝄜 J7)* **Just under an hour from Agía Nápa by bus, discover the larger town of Lárnaka (pop. 72,000).** Behind an extensive sandy beach, vibrant Cypriot life pulsates in the Old Town, its shops mainly catering to the demands of the locals. The Old Town is surrounded by a belt of residential housing and office blocks mostly built over the past 25 years. West of the fishing port and east of the oil terminal lie miles of sandy beaches, also lined by hotels.

Little remains of the ancient town of Kíti, which stood on the site of today's Lárnaka between the early Bronze Age and the early Christian era. In the Middle Ages, the importance of the town was rooted mainly in its saline lake and port.

Just follow the sea: Lárnaka's long, palm-fringed promenade

Wow!!

Magnificent iconostasis with exquisite carvings in Lazarus Church

SIGHTSEEING

OLD KÍTI

The excavation site to the northeast of town reveals the remains of a town wall and foundations of temples and copper workshops. *Mon–Wed, Fri 8am–2.30pm, Thu 8am–5pm | admission 2 euros | Makherás Street*

ARCHAEOLOGICAL DISTRICT MUSEUM

On display here are finds from Lárnaka, Choirokoitía and the villages of Pýla and Ársos, the latter the site of an ancient sanctuary devoted to Aphrodite. *Tue–Fri 8am–3pm (Thu until 5pm), Sat 9am–3pm | admission 2 euros | Kalógreon Square*

FORT

The fort at the western end of the seafront promenade was built in 1625. The photogenic courtyard features old stone anchors, cannons and cannon balls, as well as finds from excavations nearby. *Mon–Fri 9am–7.30pm (Sept–May until 5pm) | admission 2 euros | Ánkara Street, waterfront promenade*

LAZARUS CHURCH

The medieval name of the town of Lárnaka is derived from the Greek word for sarcophagus, larnax. In fact, a large number of sarcophagi have been found in Lárnaka. One of them, discovered in the 9th century, bore the inscription 'Lazarus, Friend of Christ'. The people at that time were convinced that this had to refer to the man awakened from the dead by Christ. The crypt where Lazarus was buried is still visible today below the sanctuary.

Don't miss the carvings on the iconostasis (wall). The small *church museum* in the northwest corner of the churchyard shows some pretty icons and liturgical accessories. *Mon–Fri 8.30am–12.30pm, except Wed, and 3pm–5.30pm | mu-*

seum admission 1 euro | *Ágios Lázaros Street*

PIERIDES FOUNDATION MUSEUM

Remarkable private collection housed in a 19th-century villa. On display are mainly excellent ceramics from the combed ornament ware of the Late Neolithic up to medieval exhibits. Amongst the most fascinating objects are the vessels in bichrome so-called 'free field style' from the 7th century BC. *Mon–Thu 9am–4pm, Fri and Sat 9am–1pm | admission 2 euros | Zénon Kitieus Street 4*

TURKISH QUARTER

Lying immediately west of the fort, the former Turkish quarter boasts the most important mosque in town which today is used by Arabs. A stroll through the district with its old houses gives a glimpse of the atmosphere of old Cyprus.

FOOD & DRINK

INSIDER TIP ▶ ART CAFÉ 1900

This pretty artists' café and bistro in the rooms of an old townhouse has a menu that changes daily. Along with Cypriot specialities, Oriental cakes and good ice cream are also served. The ground floor of the building features a fine bar with over 100 types of whisky. *Wed–Mon 6pm–midnight | Stasinoú Street 6, near the tourist information office | www.art cafe1900.com.cy | Budget*

MOTI MAHAL ●

Decked out in Indian style all over, this café-bar-restaurant has brought a touch of Goa to Cyprus. Whether sipping an exotic cocktail, tucking into a hot curry or enjoying a shisha pipe, sitting on a chair or cross-legged on white cushions, your eyes are always drawn to glimpses

of the sea through palm trees, all to the tune of Greek and otherworldly sounds. *Daily from noon | Athinón Street 100 | Moderate*

THE BREWERY

Crossover cuisine served in easy-going surroundings. The beer (incl. wheat beer) is produced at the in-house microbrewery. *Daily from 9am | Athinón Street 77 | Moderate*

SHOPPING

THEO MICHAEL ●

Guests are welcome at the Cypriot artist Theo Michael's Old Town studio at any time. You might just want to watch him work, admire his handiwork, take classes with him or have your portrait done in various techniques – pencil drawings for example, start at 55 euros. *Zinónos Kitiéos Street 118 | appointments tel. 24 64 88 13*

CRAFTS CENTRE

An overview of work by local craftspeople. *Kosmá Lyssiótis Street 6*

SPORTS & BEACHES

If you don't fancy taking a dip on the city beach, which boasts fine sand but is often very busy, take a bus (every half hour) leaving from Makris' bus station on Demokratias Square to the long but narrower sandy beaches west and east of the town. You'll find all kinds of water sports options in front of the hotels there.

ENTERTAINMENT

BLACK TURTLE TAVERN

This tavern is located on the first floor of an old house near Lázarus Church. *Daily* from 8pm | Fri and Sat live music from 9.30pm | Méhmet Alí Street 11 | *Budget*

CLUB TOPAZ
Mainstream, funk, Deep House and Greek hits. *Wed–Sun from 10pm | Athinón Avenue 30*

WHERE TO STAY

LIVADHIÓTIS CITY
The block of flats near Lázarus Church offers comprehensively renovated studios sleeping up to four people. *Nik. Rossos Street 50 | tel. 24 62 62 22 | www.livadhiotis.com | Budget*

PALM BEACH
This comfortable beach hotel was built some 5km (3mi) east of Lárnaka and boasts both inside and outdoor pools as well as two tennis courts and a water sports and diving centre. Handy: the scheduled buses into Lárnaka and to Agía Nápa stop right outside the door. *228 rooms | Dekeleia Road Oroklini | tel. 24 84 66 00 | www.palmbeachhotel.com | Expensive*

SUN HALL
Arguably the best city-centre hotel in Lárnaka, right on the palm-fringed waterfront promenade opposite the beach and marina. Mod cons include a heated pool, fitness room, sauna and massages. *112 rooms | Athinón Avenue 6 | tel. 24 65 33 41 | www.aquasolhotels.com.cy | Expensive*

INFORMATION

CYPRUS TOURISM ORGANISATION
Lárnaka Airport | tel. 24 00 83 68 | daily 8.15am–11pm
Vasiléos Pavloú Square | tel. 24 65 43 22 | Mon–Sat 8.15am–1.30pm, Mon, Tue, Thu, Fri also 3pm–6.15pm

8000 years ago, the Stone Age village of Choirokoitía was already inhabited

WHERE TO GO

CHOIROKOITÍA (KHIROKITIA) ⭐
(137 E3) (📖 G8)

The best-preserved of the some 50 settlements on Cyprus dated with confidence to the late Neolithic period, some 29km (18mi) southwest of Lárnaka, will astonish you. The fact that 8000 years ago people were living here in a village of stone houses comes as a surprise to western Europeans who have nothing like it at home.

The village was protected from enemies by a wall. A path leads up to the hill, opposite which you can make out remains of the wall. The round houses, some of which have been reconstructed, were built quite close to each other. The around 1000 inhabitants seem to have formed a family-like community. The largest hut had a diameter of nearly 10m. The walls were up to 3m thick. In some of the larger huts stone pillars point to the existence of a wooden intermediate storey. The building materials were raw blocks of stone, wattle and daub, as well as unfired clay bricks. *Daily 8am–5pm (June–Aug daily 8am–7.30pm) | admission 2 euros*

FATSÁ WAX MUSEUM (137 E3) (📖 G8)

At the lower entrance to the town of Skarínou, 29km (18mi) from Lárnaka, this very modern museum presents informative waxworks and has especially good displays covering more recent Cypriot history. *Daily 9am–5.30pm (May–Oct daily 9am–7pm) | admission 7 euros*

HALAN SULTAN TEKKE ⭐
(138 B5) (📖 J7)

The shore of Lárnaka's saline lake was what was once the most important Islamic sanctuary and is today the island's most popular photo motif. When the Arabs raided Cyprus for the first time back in 647, their party included a noblewoman who had known the prophet Mohammed well. At the site where the mosque stands today, she fell from her mule and died. Her grave later became a site of pilgrimage still remembered by Muslims when the Turks conquered the island in 1571. However, it took until 1816 for the Turkish governor in Cyprus to have the mosque built, which was later joined by accommodation for pilgrims.

The mosque is very plain. From the prayer room (which you mustn't enter with shoes) you reach an annexe with the dimly lit burial place of the venerated woman. *Daily 8am–6pm (Oct–May to 5pm) | free admission*

KALAVASSÓS-TÉNTA (137 D4) (📖 G8)

35km (22mi) southwest of Lárnaka, a futuristically designed roof protects the remains of a Neolithic settlement dating back 8500 years, accompanied by good information in English. *Mon–Fri 9am–4pm | admission 2 euros*

KÍTI (138 B5–6) (📖 J8)

Standing on a prettily walled square with turpentine trees at the centre of the village some 11km (7mi) south of Lárnaka, you'll come across ⭐ *Panagía Angeloktístos church*. This edifice, cobbled together from a Gothic chapel from the time of the Crusaders and a Byzantine church, was erected on the site of an Early Christian basilica. The mosaic of international importance that used to adorn the latter's vaulted apsis was integrated into the new 10th-century church building. It shows Mary with the Infant Jesus on her arm in luminescent colours on a pedestal set with precious stones against a golden background. Archangels are approaching from each side. *Mon–Sat 8am–noon and 2pm–4pm,*

Sun 9.30am–noon and 2pm–4pm | free admission

The small but pretty lighthouse 5km (3mi) southeast of Kíti on Cape Kíti dates back to British colonial times. To the east, a particularly beautiful sandy beach lines the low cliffs. Forming a narrow band past the airport nearly all the way to Lárnaka, not many tourists come here.

Designed along feng shui lines, the modern lifestyle accommodation ● 😊 INSIDER TIP *Hotel E* has a chic restaurant. The E stands for 'eco': mainly natural building materials were used and environmental issues were taken into consideration down to the small details, while in the generous spa only natural products are used *(52 rooms | Fáros Road 1 | tel. 24 74 70 00 | www.hotel-e.com | Expensive)*.

LOW BUDGET

▶ Good value on the bus: the holiday region around Agía Nápa offers the best scheduled bus connections in southern Cyprus. Commute cheaply between the towns and beaches around Agía Nápa and take cheap day trips using the regular bus service to Nicosia (15 euros return / 80 min.) and Lárnaka (10 euros / 50 min.). *EMAN | Makários Ave. 32a | Agía Nápa | tel. 23 72 13 21 | www.emantravel.com*

▶ Authentic Cypriot food, freshly prepared, is served daily between 6am and midnight at the *Vassilikís* service station, 150m before you reach the entrance to the Choirokoitía excavations: grilled pigeon for 4 euros, vegetarian main courses for 6 euros and the fish equivalent for 8–9 euros.

ÁGIOS MINÁS CONVENT
(137 D3) (𝘔 G8)

The convent in a high valley surrounded by hills, 45km (28mi) to the west, has a fortress-like character. The icons hanging in the 18th-century convent church are mostly of a more recent date, painted by the nuns here. *Daily 8am–noon and 3pm–7pm | women have to wear skirts | free admission*

STAVROVOÚNI MONASTERY ★
(137 E2) (𝘔 H7)

The oldest monastery on Cyprus stands 34km (21mi) northwest of Lárnaka on a striking conical mountain rising up 768m (2519ft) above the coastal plain. The ⚊ tarmac road leading up to the summit with plenty of hairpin bends offers splendid views of the mountains and the sea. The buildings you see today date from the 17th–18th centuries. A splinter from the Cross is said to have been worked into a silver-plated cross hanging to the right of the outermost part of the iconostasis. *Daily 8am–noon and 3pm–6pm (Sept–March 2pm–5pm) | women are not allowed in!*

NORTH CYPRUS

The best checkpoints for a daytrip to Kerýneia are in Nicosia *(p. 61)*. For a daytrip to Famagusta and onto the Karpaz peninsula by hire car or taxi you can use the checkpoint northeast of Pýla (138 C4) (𝘔 K6).

PÁNO LÉFKARA (137 D3) (𝘔 G7)

This large village in the foothills of the Tróodos mountains, some 39km (24mi) northwest of Lárnaka, is home to the hemstitching work known as *lefkarítika*. Tothether with silver jewellery, this handiwork is sold in local shops.

Girls, don't bother with this particular climb! Women are not allowed into Stavrovoúni Monastery

PÝLA ● (138 C4) (⌀ K6)

Situated in the buffer zone administered by the UN, i.e. the no-man's land between northern and southern Cyprus, this large village lies just over 8km (5mi) northeast of Lárnaka. The mosque and church each call their faithful, while some public buildings fly the Greek flag, others the Turkish. On the village square, the tavern serves a southern Cypriot beer, while the coffeehouse offers the Turkish equivalent. The owners get their fish and meat from wherever happens to be cheaper.

SALINE LAKE (138 B5) (⌀ J7)

Lárnaka's salt lake, whose shallow waters in winter usually attract flamingos, is dry in summer, but fills up again with the winter rain. *On the edge of Lárnaka*

TOCHNÍ (137 D4) (⌀ G8)

Dozens of old restored village houses some 29km (18mi) to the southwest now serve as holiday cottages. The small hotel that makes part of the complex offers a pool and an excellent restaurant. If you like, you can take part in cookery workshops and agricultural activities; riding stables and a mountain bike hire company can also be found here. *Cyprus Villages | tel. 24 33 29 98 | www.cyprusvillages.com.cy | Moderate–Expensive*

LIMASSOL

CITY **WHERE TO START?**
Old Town: If you're arriving on a municipal bus from the hotel district, get off at the central bus station, just 150m from the Old Town's market halls. Drivers will find affordable parking spaces along the four-lane seafront promenade, separated from the water by a green strip; however, you can only drive along this coming from the east. A set of traffic lights offers a chance for cars coming from the west to turn. The Old Town begins right behind the buildings lining the promenade.

Limassol (Greek: Lemesós) is a major city with over 160,000 inhabitants right by the sea and dominated by highrises (136 B5) (*DM E–F9*). To one side, while walking along the waterfront promenade, you'll nearly always see dozens of large ships in the sheltered anchorage outside the harbour waiting for a mooring space or to take on new freight. On the other side, a chain of tall office buildings in front of lofty palm trees shelters the extensive Old Town and its many buildings from the colonial era from the traffic. Large-scale regeneration work is underway to turn the Old Town into the pride and joy of Cyprus by 2015 at the latest. Here you can sit in the sun at cafés and döner bars and watch life go by, have some shoes made to measure,

Photo: The fortified tower at Kolóssi Castle

The big city makes an ideal base for easy daytrips to many important sights in southern Cyprus

stroll through the market hall and, in the evening, visit traditional music bars.

The Old Town however has some new, strong rivals. Much of local life happens along the broad motorable boulevards in the New Town, while hotels and summer nightlife draws people out to the hotel district stretching out east of the centre where holidaymakers swim at small artificially created beaches and concentrate on sunbathing by the poolside or on lawns. The curious traveller will find Limassol an ideal base for exploring, as impor-

tant historical sites and quiet mountain villages all lie within one hour's drive. Even getting to the highest peak of the island, Mount Olympus in the Tróodos mountains, or to Nicosia and Páfos won't take you much more than 90 minutes.

SIGHTSEEING

ARCHAEOLOGICAL DISTRICT MUSEUM
The small museum shows second-rate findings from the area around Limassol and Amathoús. Interesting objects of

daily use include keys from the 5th–3rd century BC. *Tue, Wed, Fri 8am–3pm, Thu 8am–5pm, Sat 9am–3pm | admission 2 euros | Cannings/corner Byron Street*

CAROB MILL ●

The prettily restored complex of a large carob mill built in 1937 not only holds many chic restaurants, cafés and a mini

MUSEUM OF MEDIEVAL CYPRUS ⚜

Alongside burial stones, armour and weapons, the 14th century castle also displays photographs of medieval buildings on Cyprus. The Gothic hall of the fortified building, from which a spiral staircase leads up on to the roof, is impressive. *Tue–Sat 9am–5pm, Sun 10am–1pm | admission 4 euros | Irinis Street*

At Governor's Beach the sun and sea reign over the beach and the snow-white cliffs

brewery, but also a vividly presented exhibition about the important role the pods of the carob tree once played on Cyprus. *Daily approx. 10am–10pm | Vasilissis Street | adjoining the castle | carob exhibition free of charge*

WINERIES

The four large wineries in Limassol, *Keo, Sodap, Etko* and *Loel,* as well as the *Keo Brewery* may be visited in the mornings. For dates and times contact the tourist information office. *All wineries lie on the road leading from the city centre to the port*

FOOD & DRINK

APOLLO GARDEN CAFÉ

This green, quiet oasis full of bits and bobs lies hidden away in the centre. Good-value snacks. *Mon–Sat 10am–6pm | Iphigenias Street 14D | Budget*

BAROLO

This gourmet restaurant has won several awards for its wines. Good salads, game, creative dishes such as foie gras in zivania. *Mon–Sat from 7pm | Odós Agíou Andréa 248 | tel. 25 76 07 67 | Expensive*

INSIDER TIP **THE OLD NEIGHBOURHOOD**

Small tavern in the Old Town that has kept its authentic charm and serves fantastic homemade fare, always fresh. In the evenings there's often music. *Mon–Sat from 5pm | Odós Ángyras (Ankaras) 14 | Budget*

INSIDER TIP **PANTOPOULÍON**

Housed in the former fish market hall, this restaurant has a large lunchtime selection of specialities, including rarities, and in the evening dishes up excellent *mesé*. Extensive selection of Cypriot wine. *Mon–Sat 11.30am–3.30pm and 7pm–midnight | Fri and Sat evenings live Greek music | between Kanáris and Athens Street | lunchtime Budget | dinner Moderate*

SHOPPING

BEAR FACTORY

These teddy bears are actually manufactured here, also according to customers' specification. *Kóstas Partassídis Street 34 | New Town*

BOUKLA BOUKLA

Hip young women's fashion and accessories from the studios of three young Greek designers. *Ágios Andréas Street 252 | Old Town*

MARKET HALLS

The most interesting market halls in the south of the island were modernised in 2001 and sell fish, fruit and veg, as well as baskets and Cypriot specialities. *Mon–Fri 6am–2.30pm (Wed only until 1.15pm), Sat 6am–1.30pm | between Kanáris and Athens Street*

ORPHEUS ART GALLERY

Modern painting and ceramics from Greece and Cyprus. *Athens Street 291 | Old Town*

SPORTS & BEACHES

Only locals swim from the beaches of Limassol. The hotels to the west of the city have small sandy beaches. Prettier options are the long *Lady Mile Beach* at the salt lake, as well as wide *Koúrion Beach.* The most charming has got to be INSIDER TIP Governor's Beach (136 D4) (*Ø G9*) with small sandy beaches in front of green sunbathing lawns and tiny sandy or pebbly spots below the white cliffs.

ENTERTAINMENT

INSIDER TIP **ELLINÁDIKO**

Trendy music bar catering mainly to younger Greeks who like to dance to Greek instead of international rock music. *Fri/Sat from 11pm | Ifigénias Street 6*

LEMESIANÉS VRADIÉS

Mesé restaurant in the Old Town in an former residential building. Musicians

---

MARCO POLO HIGHLIGHTS

★ **Fasoúri**
Cypress avenue running through this vitamin-rich paradise → p. 49

★ **Kolóssi Castle**
Fortified sugarcane factory between fields and plantations → p. 49

★ **Koúrion**
Koúrion has the only temple on Cyprus. And from the seating of the ancient amphitheatre you can see both the stage and the sea → p. 50

move from table to table playing Greek songs. The majority of the punters tend to be locals. *Daily from 7pm | tel. 25 35 33 78 | Irínis Street 111 | Expensive*

Zaímis Street 13 | tel. 25 58 28 50 | www. lordoshotelapts.com | Budget

WHERE TO STAY

CURIUM PALACE
Best city-centre hotel boasting colonial flair in a classy 1950s building. Outdoor pool, small indoor pool, gym, spa. *62 rooms | Byron Street 11 | tel. 25 89 11 00 | www.curiumpalace.com | Expensive*

H.H. GRAND RESORT
Luxury hotel with a palm-fringed pool plus an indoor pool, spa and fitness centre, with their own watersports and diving station. You can choose from six restaurants and every evening there are folklore shows. *255 rooms | Old Lefkosía-Lemesós Road | Amathus Area | tel. 25 63 43 33 | www.grandresort.com. cy | Expensive*

LÓRDOS HOTEL APARTMENTS
Modern studios and flats for 2–4 people in a four-storey house in a street parallel to the waterfront, some 20 minutes from the Old Town and some 3 minutes from the nearest small beach. Some of the studios have balconies. Air-conditioning is charged separately. *23 rooms | Andréa*

INFORMATION

CYPRUS TOURISM ORGANISATION
Spýrou Araoúzou Avenue 115 A | tel. 25 36 27 56; George A' Street 35 | Germasógeia, in the hotel district | tel. 25 32 32 11 | both Mon–Sat 8.15am–1.30pm, Mon, Tue, Thu, Fri also 3pm–6.15pm

WHERE TO GO

INSIDER TIP AKROTÍRI
(136 A6) (ØD E10)
The *Akrotíri Environmental Information Centre* on the main street *(daily 8.30am– 3pm | free admission)* 15km (9mi) south-west of Limassol has brief information on the natural environment and gives hints for bird-watching. Between November and April you can watch the flamingos in the salt lake of Akrotíri through binoculars from the ✲ roof.

OLD AMATHOÚS (136 C4) (ØD F9)
In antiquity parts of today's hotel town, 9km (5½mi) further east, were occupied by the city kingdom of Amathoús. In a similar way to Kíti, today's Lárnaka, it was influenced by the Phoenicians up to the middle of the first pre-Christian

RUSSIANS IN LIMASSOL

These days, Russian has become as important in Limassol as English. You'll see menus and signs in Cyrillic here, and the rouble is rolling in. Limassol is basically a huge money-laundering operation. Many Russians have invested their illicit income in newly-founded offshore companies to invest the freshly laundered money back again to the former Soviet states. At least on paper, small Cyprus has become the most important investor in Russia, even ahead of the US, Holland and Germany.

Vitamin C: lemons, kiwis and avocados thrive in the plantations in Fasoúri

millennium. However, there is hardly anything left of the ancient city. East of Amathus Beach Hotel, on the left-hand side of the road, the remains of the Agorá and an Early Christian basilica may be visited. *Daily 9am–5pm (June–Aug 9am–7.30pm) | admission 1.70 euros*

AVDÍMOU (135 E6) (*ω D9*)

These two beaches in Avdímou, completely unspoilt by buildings, are situated on the sovereign territory of the British military base – some 35km (22mi) west of Limassol. Narrow roads lead from the old state road to Melanda Beach, some 150m long, as well as to INSIDERTIP Avdímou Beach with its recommendable *Kyrénia tavern (Budget)*.

EPISKOPÍ (136 A5) (*ω E9*)

The small Archaeological Museum in the large village some 12km (7½mi) west of Limassol shows some finds from Koúrion in a rather colonial atmosphere *(Mon–Fri 8am–4pm, Thu until 5pm | well signposted | admission 2 euros)*.

ERÍMI (136 A5) (*ω E9*)

The well-signed private ● *Cyprus Wine Museum* on the road leading from Limassol to Episkopí (15km/9mi) explains the cultivation and production of wine on the island. Wine tastings are also held in this pleasant building and wine can be bought *(daily 9am–5pm, closed on public holidays | admission incl. wine tasting 5 euros)*.

FASOÚRI ★ (136 A5) (*ω E9*)

To the southwest of Limassol a lush plantation landscape awaits you, crossed by a cypress-lined avenue that goes on for miles. Lemons, oranges, grapefruit, avocados and kiwis thrive here.

KOLÓSSI ★ (136 A5) (*ω E9*)

On the northwest edge of the plantations of Fasoúri, some 12km (7½mi) from Limassol, the brown ⚘ fortified tower of Kolóssi castle juts up between cypress trees. Its roof affords far-reaching views. *Kolóssi Castle* used to belong to the Knights Hospitaller crusaders, which

And the sea provides the stage set: Koúrion's ancient amphitheatre dates back to the 2nd century AD

had its headquarters here up until 1309 and, after being moved to Rhodes, administered its Cyprus estates from Kolóssi. Sugarcane and grapes were grown here, the latter producing the sweet fortified wine called *commandaría*.

A massive tree which stands on the eastern side of the castle, marks the end of a medieval aqueduct. The water brought in on the aqueduct powered the mill wheels used to squeeze the juice from the sugar cane. The production of the sugar proper then took place in the adjacent hall-like building. *Daily 9am–5pm (June–Aug 8am–7.30pm) | admission 2 euros*

KOÚRION ★ 〰️ (135 F6) (🕮 D9)

Stretching across a plateau some 15km (9mi) west of Limassol, this is the most important archaeological site on the southern coast after Páfos. The best course of action is to start your visit with one of the highlights of the compound, the *Sanctuary of Apollo Hylates* on the former western edge of town. In the holy area you'll see the foundation walls of several rooms used by pilgrims, the priest's house and Roman thermal baths,

as well as a partly reconstructed temple dating back to the 1st century AD.

On your way from the Apollo sanctuary towards Limassol you'll pass the *Roman stadium* which used to hold some 6000 spectators on seven rows of seats, of which a small part has been restored.

In the excavations of the town of Koúrion (entrance 4km (2½mi) from the Apollo sanctuary) you should first visit the impressive 〰️ *ancient amphitheatre*, which was laid out in the shape we see today in the 2nd century AD and used to hold 3500 spectators.

Apart from the theatre make sure you see the *mosaics* in the *House of Eustolios*, particularly interesting to archaeologists as they actually date from Christian times – from the early 5th century. At the time, it wasn't common practice to show representations of biblical scenes and saints; instead, birds and geometrical patterns were chosen. Inscriptions on the floor include mentions of Christ.

Like most of these mosaics, the large *basilica* at the other end of the Koúrion excavations also dates from the 5th century, when the change from pagan to Christian Koúrion took place. With five naves, the basilica was an impressive display of splendour, evidenced by remains of floor mosaics, roof tiles and the fountains in two forecourts.

Opposite the basilica are the extensive ruins of the *Acropolis* which represented the city-centre so to speak of ancient Koúrion. Together with many foundations and the remains of the thermal baths with a complex of fountains called the *nymphaeum*, look out for three Roman floor mosaics near the fence on the main street. One shows gladiators fighting, one the rape of Ganymede by Zeus in the guise of an eagle, a third Odysseus discovering Achilles hidden by his mother Thetis on Skíros. *Daily 8am–5pm (June–Aug until 7.30pm) | entrance to Apollo sanctuary 2 euros, Koúrion 2 euros*

LÓFOU (135 F5) (*M D8*)

24km (15mi) northwest of Limassol, this large mountain village with its many narrow alleyways is among the most beautiful in the south of the island. Cypriots and most of all British expats have carefully restored many of the old village houses. Only at the height of summer and at weekends is there much going on here. A good choice for a place to stay and eat among the natural-stone walls of this historic village is INSIDER TIP *I Lófou (daily from noon | 6 rooms | tel. 25 47 02 02 | www.lofou-agrovino.com | Moderate)*.

PISSOÚRI (135 D6) (*M C9*)

Pissoúri is divided into two: the old village is high up on a hill, some 39km (24mi) west of Limassol, while the small holiday resort of Pissoúri Beach can be found 3km (less than 2mi) away on a long sandy and pebbly beach. In the mountain village you can still enjoy traditional rural life and at the seaside a relatively unspoilt stretch of coastline.

This makes Pissoúri an ideal choice for a quiet holiday in the south of the island away from the trappings of mass tourism. In the old mountain village, simple rural accommodation is provided at the INSIDER TIP *Bunch of Grapes Inn (11 rooms | tel. 25 33 12 75 | bogpisouri@hotmail.com | Budget)*. The rooms are on the top floor of an old farmhouse that's over 100 years old and has a flower-filled courtyard. In the garden and ground floor a restaurant spoils residents and non-residents alike with fine fare *(daily from 7pm | Expensive)*. Every Wednesday between June and September the three tavernas on the village square stage a ● INSIDER TIP *Cypriot evening* with plenty of folklore. Many villagers join visitors for this.

Right on the sea, the luxurious ☺ *Columbia Beach Resort* suite hotel (with a 80m-laguna pool) was built using organic building materials and has been integrated into the coastal landscape as a model of sustainable development *(tel. 25 83 30 00 | www.columbia-hotels.com | Expensive)*.

LOW BUDGET

▶ For inexpensive made-to-measure shoes in Limassol, head for Jámi Street near the castle, such as to *Made to Measure Shoes by Lydia | Jámi Street 14*

▶ Free sightseeing: as in all towns in southern Cyprus, the *Cyprus Tourism Organisation* in Limassol offers free guided tours in English. In the winter the schedule also features free bus tours with walks in the surrounding area. Information: → p. 48

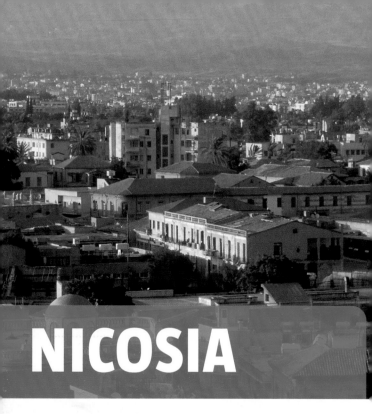

NICOSIA

CITY WHERE TO START?

Old Town: scheduled buses arrive at Platía Dion Solomoú next to the city wall. Right next to it, there is a pay-and-display car park on Tripoli Bastion. Further car parks (not free) accessible from Leofóros Omiroú and Leofóros Stasinoú, are in the ditch area along the city wall. Even visitors arriving by shared taxi should ask to be dropped off at the city wall, e.g. at the beginning of Lídra Street. Bear in mind that apart from the Cyprus Museum, all sights in Nicosia are located in the Old Town.

MAP INSIDE BACK COVER

In Nicosia (131 E4) (*G–H5*), the mad course of history is all around you. For a start, the city (pop. 210,000) has three names: in Greek it's Lefkosía and in Turkish Lefkoşa, while Venetians and the British called it Nicosia.

The Old Town of Nicosia, perfectly preserved within its nearly 500 years old city walls, is divided into two halves by sandbags and rusty oil barrels. You might be ambling along a pedestrianised main shopping street and have to show your ID halfway down because you're crossing a border called the 'Green Line', which Turkey is the only state in the world to recognise. In the *Berlin No. 2* snack bar, Greek-Cypriot soldiers lean their guns on the counter when they come over for a

Photo: Nicosia – view of the Kerýneia Mountains and Selimiye Mosque

Sharp division: since southern Cyprus joined the EU, you can roam all over Nicosia even though the capital still remains divided

coffee; in the main mosque in the north the prayer mats have been placed at an angle because the prayer niche had to be fitted into the walls of a Gothic cathedral to point towards Mecca. Still, you won't really feel gloomy here, as the people have adapted to the madness and life takes its gentle course. The surroundings however conjure up a bizarre feeling: on a clear day, seen from Nicosia, the two mountain ranges of the island with their medieval castles, churches and monasteries appear close enough to touch.

However, in Turkey's opinion, these, too, lie in two separate states.

In 2017 Nicosia wants to become European Capital of Culture – by then the Old Town on either side of the border is supposed to be spruced up even more, with many more historic buildings put to good use again. The first small Old Town quarter to be restored back in the 1980s and turned into a nightlife district, was *Laikí Gitoniá* in the Greek-Cypriot part.

A reminder of the end of British rule: Freedom Monument

SIGHTSEEING

ÁGIOS GIANNIS CATHEDRAL
(U E4) (𝄞 e4)

The city's Orthodox cathedral is a surprisingly small edifice, built in 1662 on the ruins of a Crusader church. The interior was completely painted between 1736 and 1756. *Mon–Sat 8am–noon and Mon–Fri 2pm–4pm | free admission | Archbishop Kiprianós Square | southern Nicosia*

ARABAHMET MOSQUE (U B3) (𝄞 b3)

This mosque in the INSIDER TIP Old Town quarter bearing its name – and well worth exploring – is considered the most beautiful, Islamic, sacred building in Nicosia. Dating from the 17th century, it was named after one of the officers who participated in the Ottoman conquest of Cyprus in 1571. Also take a look at the fine Muslim cemetery with its old tombs. *Freely accessible outside prayer times | Sehit Salahi Şevket Cad. | northern Nicosia*

BANK OF CYPRUS CULTURAL FOUNDATION ● (U C4) (𝄞 c4)

Art objects from the 2nd century BC to the Middle Ages, presented in a pleasingly modern way. Restaurant *(Moderate)* on the upper floor. *Daily 10am–7pm | free admission | Phaneroménis Street 86–90 | southern Nicosia | www.boccf.org*

BÜYÜK HAMAM (U C3) (𝄞 c3)

The 'Great Turkish Bath', installed by the Ottomans in a Catholic church from the Middle Ages, reopened in 2010 after a 2-year restoration period. *Büyük Han Cad. | northern Nicosia*

BÜYÜK HAN ★ (U C3) (𝄞 c3)

Founded in 1572 straight after the conquest of Cyprus by the Ottomans, the 'Great Caravanserai' has been completely restored. The place where once traders bedded down with mules and camels is now occupied by a very atmospheric café restaurant, craft shops and small galleries. *Closed Sun | entrances Arasta Sok. and Kurtbaba Sok. | northern Nicosia*

ARCHIEPISCOPAL PALACE
(U E4) (𝄞 e4)

With the independence of Cyprus in 1960, Makários III had an extensive palace built for himself in the Old Town.

This was where he resided until 1977 as archbishop and president of the state at the same time. *No visits of the interior | Archbishop Kiprianós Square | southern Nicosia*

ETHNOGRAPHICAL MUSEUM ●
(U E4) (⌘ e4)

The ethnographical museum is housed in the former archiepiscopal palace. One of the collections' focal points is technical equipment from the time before industrialisation. On display are traditional costumes and woven pieces, hemstitching from Páno Léfkara and beautifully carved wooden chests, jewellery and household items, icons and naïve paintings. *Mon–Fri 9.30am–4pm | admission 2 euros | Archbishop Kiprianós Square | southern Nicosia*

FAMAGUSTA GATE (U F4) (⌘ f4)

The city gate from Venetian times serves as an arts centre where exhibitions, concerts, theatre performances and other events take place. The gate, called Porta Giuliana by the Venetians, consists of a 35m-long corridor leading from the city into the wall ditch. Left and right of the corridor is where the guards had their quarters. *Mon–Fri 10am–1pm and 4pm–7pm (May–Sept 5pm–8pm) | free admission | Nikifóros Phókas Avenue | southern Nicosia*

FREEDOM MONUMENT
(U E–F5) (⌘ e–f5)

This large modern monument with the many bronze figures on the city wall opposite the New Archiepiscopal Palace shows the liberation of the Cypriot people from British colonial domination by EOKA freedom fighters. It is crowned by a statue representing freedom. *Nikifóros Phókas Avenue | southern Nicosia*

HOUSE OF HADJIYORGÁKIS KORNÉSIOS (U E5) (⌘ e5)

This museum shows how a wealthy Greek in 18th century Cyprus would have lived. Between 1779 and 1809 Hadjiyorgákis Kornésios lived in this house with his family. During that time he had the title of Dragoman, the top Christian administrative civil servant on the island. Being in charge of collecting taxes from the Christians for the Christian church and the Turkish sultan, he was at the same time considered a spokesperson for his fellow Christians as somebody who had direct access to the sultan at all times. *Sat 9.30am–3.30pm, Tue, Wed, Fri 8.30am–3pm, Thu 8.30–5pm | admission 2 euros | Patriarch Gregórios Street | southern Nicosia*

ICONS MUSEUM ★ ● (U E4) (*m e4*)

Housed in two rooms in a wing of the New Archiepiscopal Palace, this museum has over 100 of the most beautiful and valuable Cypriot icons and mosaics, ranging from the 8th to the 18th century. The collection provides a thorough overview of the various different styles, western influences and the thematic range of Byzantine art. *Mon–Fri 9am–4.30pm, Sat 9am–1pm | admission 4 euros | Archbishop Kiprianós Square | southern Nicosia*

KUMARCILAR HAN (U C3) (*m c3*)

The 17th century 'Caravanserai of the Gamblers' is little more but a ruin today. Passing traders once used to find accommodation here in 52 rooms. *Asma Alti Sok. | northern Nicosia*

LAIKÍ GITONIÁ ★ (U C5) (*m c5*)

Many houses in the Old Town could do with urgent renovation work. In a small part the city has done exactly that: Laikí Gitoniá. From 1984 a romantic corner has been created here, with several atmospheric taverns and a few souvenir shops. This is where you'll find that Mediterranean atmosphere everybody looks for and enjoys on holiday. *Between Regaena and Hippocrates Street | southern Nicosia*

LEVENDIS MUSEUM (U C5) (*m c5*)

This museum on the edge of Laikí Gitoniá presents documents and objects illustrating life in Nicosia over the past three millennia. *Tue–Sun 10am–4.30pm | free admission | Hippocrates Street | southern Nicosia | www.leventismuseum.org.cy*

MEVLEVI TEKKE MUSEUM (U C1–2) (*m c1–2*)

Together with Turkish crafts, this former monastery of the Turkish Dervish order shows mainly musical instruments and costumes of the 'Whirling Dervishes'. The brotherhood which has its headquarters in the Turkish town of Konya, was banned by Kemal Atatürk. *Daily 9am–1pm and 2pm–5pm, Nov–April only 9am–2pm | admission 5 YTL | Girne Cad. | northern Nicosia*

LÍDRAS STREET (U C4–5) (*m c4–5*)

The Old Town's main drag for strolling and shopping, lined by many cafés and restaurants, leads to a checkpoint where EU citizens and all Cypriots may cross the Green Line without any problems. A colourful bazaar district can be found on the other side.

MOTORBIKE MUSEUM (U B4) (*m b4*)

Over 150 motorbikes from the period between 1914 and 1983. *Mon–Fri 9.30am–1.30pm and 3pm–7pm, Sat 9am–1pm | admission 5 euros | Graníkou Street 44 | www.agrino.org/motormuseum*

NATIONAL STRUGGLE MUSEUM ● (U E4) (*m e4*)

As the name suggests, here you will find shattering testimonies from the fight for independence from the British colonial power. *Mon–Fri 8am–2pm, Thu except in July/Aug also 3pm–5.30pm | free admission | Archbishop Kiprianós Square | southern Nicosia*

OBSERVATORIUM ⚞ (U C5) (*m c5*)

From the 11th floor of the Ermes highrise on Lídras Street you can see all of Nicosia. *June–Aug daily 10am–8pm, Nov–March daily 9.30am–5pm | admission 1 euro | entrance in Arsinóis Street | southern Nicosia*

The Venetians built the city wall around Nicosia. One way through was Famagusta Gate

OMERIYE BATHS ● (U D4) (𝄞 d4)

Today, the Turkish hamam, or Turkish Bath, is an atmospheric spa centre. *Admission 20 euros, otherwise no visits of the interior possible | Tillýrias Square | southern Nicosia*

SELIMIYE MOSQUE/SOPHIA CATHEDRAL ★ (U D3) (𝄞 d3)

Nicosia's main mosque today was built between 1208 and 1236 as a Gothic cathedral to crown the French-born kings of Cyprus. The Gothic lancet windows and tracery are very well preserved, only the interior was stripped of all pictorial representation according to Islamic doctrine. *Freely accessible outside prayer times | Arasta Sok. | northern Nicosia*

CITY WALLS

The city walls from Venetian times, today marked over long stretches by a road, used to be fortified by eleven bastions. Originally there were only three gates: Famagusta Gate (U F4) (𝄞 f4), Páfos Gate (U B4) (𝄞 b4) in the west and Kerýneia Gate (U C1) (𝄞 c1) in the north. The broad wall ditch is still easily discernible, despite the sports facilities and car parks that have been established here.

CYPRUS MUSEUM ★ (U A–B5) (𝄞 a–b5)

The 16 rooms of this pleasantly compact museum, built by the British in the early 20th century, shows the most beautiful and valuable finds made by archaeologists on Cyprus. You'll need about two hours to get an overview of the cultural development of the island from the late Neolithic to the early Middle Ages.

Room 1 shows that the people nearly 8000 years ago had the same fundamental needs as we have now.

Sculptures in Cyprus Museum

You see objects imported from Athens, Crete and Mycenae. Showpieces of local pottery are two 7th century vases in the 'free-field' style. One shows a bull sniffing an opened lotus blossom, the other a stylised bird holding a fish in its long beak.

Room 4 houses some of the around 2000 votive figures that were found in an ancient sanctuary on the northern coast. They are presented the way they were found by archaeologists in the soil. The smallest are only 10 cm high, while some reach life size. The human figures have such individual features that they might represent portraits of the benefactors who were hoping for divine protection by leaving their statue behind.

Rooms 5 and *6* look at the development of large-scale sculpture on Cyprus. Particularly impressive are the archaic lions from Tamassós. *Room 7* unites numerous objects to do with Cyprus' main source of income in Antiquity: copper – amongst them copper bars from the Bronze Age in the shape of stretched oxen skins, and cult figures from copper such as the famous Horned God of Enkomi and the 'Ingot God' standing on a copper ingot armed with a spear.

Room 8 shows reconstructions of burial rites of the people in the late Neolithic to the 5th century BC. In *Room 9* you'll see burial tombs from the 6th–3rd century BC. *Room 10* presents the development of Cypriot script, and *Room 11* displays finds from the royal tombs of Sálamis. Worth seeing too is the ivory work on the royal furniture and a large bronze kettle on an iron trivet from the early 8th century.

In *Room 12* several dioramas present the methods of extracting and processing copper in Antiquity. *Room 13* shows Roman statues brought here from Sá-

Cross-shaped idols made of andesite, probably carried like amulets, were supposed to protect their owners from supernatural evils. Necklaces such as the ones on display made from shells and carnelian were worn as jewellery. Stone bowls as well as clay jars were used in the household. This early pottery, 6000 years old, illustrates how humans were already creating pretty objects for everyday use: bowls and jars were polished red and painted, and often decorated with wavy lines that were etched into the still wet paint with a comb-like tool, which has earned this early type the name of 'pattern-combed ware'. *Room 2* tells of life in the early Bronze Age. Three pretty terracotta models show temple scenes and farmers ploughing. *Room 3* presents the further history of Cypriot ceramics in 'fast-forward' mode.

lamis. *Room 14* finally uses small objects to remind the visitor of the prehistoric world. You can see chariot models that may have served as children's toys, and terracotta figures of women in childbirth. *Tue, Wed, Fri 8am–4pm, Thu 8am–5pm, Sat 9am–4pm, Sun 10am–1pm | admission 4 euros | Museum Street 1 | southern Nicosia*

FOOD & DRINK

In southern Nicosia nearly all taverns of interest to tourists are situated in the restored *Laikí Gitoniá* Old Town district, while in northern Nicosia they cluster around *Atatürk Square*.

INSIDER TIP ▸ AEGEON
(U F3) (*ⓜ f3*)

Restaurant with pleasant atmosphere near Famagusta Gate; excellent à la carte *mesé*. Make sure you make a telephone reservation. *Daily from 8pm | tel. 22 43 32 97 | Hector Street 40 | southern Nicosia | Expensive*

INSIDER TIP ▸ BOGHJALIAN KONAK ●
(U B3) (*ⓜ b3*)

Classically styled rooms in the former house of an Armenian draper, pretty courtyard, mainly grilled food. *Mon–Sat noon–4pm and from 7pm, bar daily 11am–midnight | Salahi Şevket Sok. | northern Nicosia | www.boghjalian.com | Moderate*

FRIDAY'S (U B5) (*ⓜ b5*)

This eatery is an American-style bar, cocktail bar and restaurant on two floors. Cross-over cuisine, tasty smoothies, excellent *Long Island tea*. *Daily from midday | Diágorou Street 12 | southern Nicosia | Expensive*

MATTHEOS ● (U D4) (*ⓜ d4*)

This simple tavern near Faneromeni Church offers a large selection of basic authentic Cypriot dishes, such as stew and sweet potatoes with pork. *Mon–Sat 10am–5pm | Lefkónos Street | southern Nicosia | Budget*

INSIDER TIP ▸ SEDIR CAFÉ
(U C3) (*ⓜ c3*)

In terms of atmosphere and fabulous food, there's no eatery in northern Nicosia that comes close to this one in the pretty courtyard of the Great Caravanserai. Everything here is homemade; you may watch the rolling out of the dough for the ravioli and dumplings in the morning. Our recommendation: ravioli filled with meat or cheese, followed by yoghurt with honey, all washed down with a glass of *ayran*. *Mon, Thu 9am–8pm, Sat 9am–4pm, Tue, Wed and Fri (with live music) to midnight | Büyük Han | Budget*

LOW BUDGET

▸ Low-price Old Town rooms: a relatively cheap option for backpackers and other travellers yet with acceptable conditions, is *Tony B & B* guesthouse on the edge of Laikí Gitoniá. *Solónos St. 13 | tel. 22 66 77 94 | Budget*

▸ Old Town bus: to get a first impression of southern Nicosia's Old Town, hop on the free scheduled bus no. 1, which during the week leaves every 30 minutes from Platía Eleftherías for a 45-minute tour.

XEFOTO (U C5) *(ⓜ c5)*

In the evening, this place attracts many Cypriots. English-speaking host Andreas dishes up a *mesé* and wine on draught; guests sing and dance to live Greek music (from 9.30pm) – and often the host joins in too. *Daily from 11am | Laikí Gitoniá | southern Nicosia | Moderate*

SHOPPING

Southern Nicosia's main shopping drags are *Lídras* and *Onásgoras Street* in the Old Town, as well as *Makários Avenue* in the New Town. You'll find plenty of souvenir shops in the Old Town district of *Laikí Gitoniá*. In the other part of town, in northern Nicosia, *Arasta Sok.* (U C–D3) *(ⓜ c–d3)* forms the main shopping street of the Turkish-Cypriot Old Town.

MARKETS

Much more interesting than the market hall (U D4) *(ⓜ d4)* in southern Nicosia's Old Town *(daily 7.30am–1pm | Platía Dimarchías)* are the INSIDER TIP Wednesday Market on the Constanza Bastion of the city wall (U D5–6) *(ⓜ d5–6) (daily 6am–5pm)* and the market hall in northern Nicosia's Old Town (U D3) *(ⓜ d3)*, which you'll find in the direct vicinity of the Selimiye Mosque.

STATE CRAFTS CENTRE (O) *(ⓜ O)*

Sales exhibition with fixed prices; some craftspeople have their workshop here too. *Mon–Fri 7.30am–2.30pm, Thu (apart from July/Aug) also 3pm–6pm | Athalássia Street 186 | near the Lárnaka/Limassol motorway | southern Nicosia*

ENTERTAINMENT

ENALLAX (U F3) *(ⓜ f3)*

A place for music lovers – Wed: Classic Rock, Thu–Sat live Greek music. *Leofóros Athínas | just before the Green Line | Wed–Sat from 11pm*

WHERE TO STAY

CENTRUM (U C5) *(ⓜ c5)*

This new and modern hotel occupies a very central position on the edge of the Old Town quarter of Laikí Gitoniá. Free internet access. Very friendly staff. *40 rooms | Pasikratous Street 15 | southern Nicosia | tel. 22 45 64 44 | www.centrum hotel.net | Moderate*

CITY ROYAL (O) *(ⓜ O)*

This modern hotel near the long-distance bus station outside the Old Town boasts a rooftop terrace, indoor pool, Turkish baths, nightclub and casino. Excellent value for money. *86 rooms | Kemal Asik Cad. 19 | | northern Nicosia | tel. 2 28 76 21 | www.city-royal.com | Moderate*

CLASSIC (U B4) *(ⓜ b4)*

Modern hotel with tasteful interior and intimate character. Right on the city wall near Páfos Gate. *57 rooms | Régaena Street 94 | southern Nicosia | tel. 22 66 40 06 | www.classic.com.cy | Expensive*

HOLIDAY INN (U B5) *(ⓜ b5)*

The Old Town's most comfortable hotel is next to the city wall. Indoor pool, non-smokers floors, gym. *140 rooms | Régaena Street 70 | southern Nicosia | tel. 22 71 27 12 | hinnicres@cytanet.com.cy | Expensive*

INSIDER TIP SKY (U C5) *(ⓜ c5)*

Basic rooms with small balconies; very central location in Laiki Gitonia. *24 rooms | Solónos Street 7 C | tel. 22 66 68 80 | www.skyhotel.ws | Budget*

INFORMATION

CYPRUS TOURISM ORGANISATION (U C5) ( c5)
Laikí Gitoniá | southern Nicosia | tel. 22 67 42 64 | Mon–Fri 8.30am–4pm, Sat 8.30am–2pm

NORTH CYPRUS TOURIST INFORMA-TION (U C1) ( c1)
Kerýneia Gate | tel. 2 27 29 94

CROSSINGS BETWEEN NORTHERN AND SOUTHERN NICOSIA (CHECK-POINTS)

Ledra Palace checkpoint (U A2) ( a2):
right on the edge of the Old Town, only a ten minute walk from the city centres of both sections of the island's capital. Ledra Palace checkpoint is open round the clock. You may cross it on foot, by bike, hire car or taxi. There are taxis at all times on both sides. If you're coming from the south by taxi and with luggage, you can pass the Green Line on foot here and then continue your journey with a cheaper Turkish-Cypriot taxi on the other side.

Ágios Dométios checkpoint (O) ( O):
the 24-hour checkpoint in the western New Town near the horse racetrack of southern Nicosia is so far from either city centre that you should only pass it by hire car or taxi.

Lídras Street checkpoint (U C4) ( c4):
central location in the Old Town, pedestrians only, open around the clock.

WHERE TO GO

ASINOÚ ★ (130 A5) ( E6)
Medieval monks were looking for solitude. So they settled at the upper end of a valley on the edge of the Tróodos Mountains between forests and pastures,

Browsing, buying, sipping coffee: shops and cafés in Nicosia's shopping streets

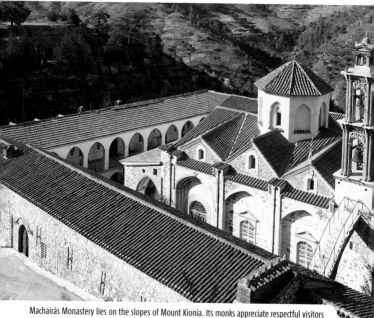

Machairás Monastery lies on the slopes of Mount Kionía. Its monks appreciate respectful visitors

30km (19mi) southwest. Of their *Panagía Forviótissa* monastery in the Asinoú township only the church remains; the residential and farm buildings made of wood and clay have disappeared. However, the church is one of the largest art treasures in Cyprus. From the outside, the small, single-naved edifice with its low brick roof resembles a barn more than a church. Look closely and you'll discover a second older barrel vault under the brick construction below the nave and domes above the porch. The brick roof was probably an inspiration borrowed from Crusader architecture, later to be placed over the building like a hood for protection against the elements. For this reason, the wall paintings inside have been preserved so well. The oldest date back to 1105/06 – and now, after being cleaned 25 years ago, the colours

are nearly as strong as they were some 900 years previously.

The key to the church is held by the village priest of Nikitári, a village near Asinoú. He's usually in the church until 4pm, otherwise in the village; a donation is expected

FIKÁRDOU (130 C6) (*M F7*)

This small village near Machairás Monastery has been listed in its entirety since 1978. Only a dozen people live here permanently, 40km (25mi) southwest of the capital. The state has had many houses restored in the original style of the 18th and 19th centuries, so that Fikárdou can today be considered a museum village. Most houses, built of rough stone and clay, have two storeys. Two of them are now used as a ethnographical and agricultural museum with a photographic

shop the nuns sell cheap printed icons and homemade marzipan. *Open daytime (rest period noon–3pm) | free admission*

MACHAIRÁS (MAKHERÁS) MONASTERY (136 C2) (⌂ F7)

A bendy narrow road leads from Mesaória over 900m (2950ft) up through the dense forests on the slopes of Mount Kioniá – 32km (20mi) southwest of Nicosia, to ⚲ *Panagía Machairás* Monastery. Founded back in the 12th century, the buildings you see today, including the church in the narrow monastery yard, date from when the monastery was rebuilt in 1892 following a fire. The walls in the church were decorated with paintings in the Byzantine style in the 1990s. Today, the monks still living here are not so keen to receive non-Orthodox visitors anymore, as too fee people show any respect. *Groups Mon, Tue and Thu 9am–noon | free admission*

documentation on former village life and the restoration work, as well as old furniture and tools *(museums April–Oct daily 9am–5pm, Nov–March daily 8am–4pm | admission 2 euros)*. You can also get very good food in the village pub *(Budget)* opposite the church.

ÁGIOS IRAKLÍDIOS CONVENT (131 D6) (⌂ G6)

Like the royal tombs of Tamassós, the convent lies in the immediate vicinity of the small dying village of *Politikó* on the edge of Mesaória, 21km (13mi) from the capital towards the southwest. Nuns have been living here since 1962 in a Garden of Eden of their own planting. Visitors are usually more fascinated by the convent's garden-like courtyard than by the building. Swifts build their nests in the cloisters and in the small convent

TAMASSÓS (131 D6) (⌂ G6)

Before you reach the small village of *Politikó* (some 19km/12mi southwest of Nicosia), a sign points to the *Royal Tombs*. Mentioned from the Iron Age onwards and famous in Antiquity for its rich copper resources, most of the town of Tamassós still lies buried underground; only a few foundation walls of a temple dedicated to Aphrodite Astarte and a few workshops have been exposed. The two graves from the 6th century BC are interesting because they imitate real buildings. Built into the soil, the graves have limestone ceilings. The ceiling beams, doorframes, fake doors and windows, window balustrades and abutments at the entrance appear to have been modelled on Egypt and the Middle East. *April–Oct daily 9.30am–5pm, Nov–March daily 8.30am–4pm | admission 2 euros*

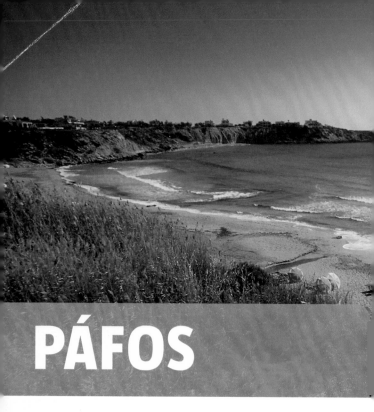

PÁFOS

(134 B5) *(𝄞 A–B8)* **The west of the island is more sparsely populated than the rest of southern Cyprus. The largest town in the region, Páfos (Paphos in English, pop. 40,000), has retained its friendly small-town character, while the second-largest, Pólis, is little more than a village.**

It was only in the mid-1980s that tourism overtook agriculture and most hotels show that they were built at a time of increasing awareness for environmental issues.

The climate in the west of the island is milder and more temperate, so that even bananas can be grown around Páfos. Apart from all kinds of fruit, peanuts thrive here too. On the slopes inland from the coast there are many olive groves and carob trees, with a lot of wine being produced in the mountains.

With hardly any industry, the natural environment has remained mostly intact. The Páfos district has plenty of forests and the Akamás peninsula in the far west of Cyprus is nearly devoid of people. Turtles lay their eggs on its sandy beaches and wonderful hiking trails lead through parts of this untouched scenery.

The area around Páfos is also a region imbued with history. In Antiquity, Páfos was an important city kingdom with a world-famous pilgrims' sanctuary dedicated to Aphrodite; in Ptolemean and Roman times, governors ruled the whole island from their base in Páfos. History marks the appearance of Páfos to this day: taverns and hotels stand right next

Photo: Coral Bay Beach

Paradise under threat:
the still intact nature in the west of the island
relies on gentle tourism

to the ancient and medieval buildings that are spread across the entire town. In the most beautiful (and most expensive) taverns, those on the fishing harbout, you're sitting exactly where 2000 years ago pilgrims came to shore, ships were built from the cedar wood from the forests and the natural resources of Cyprus were put aboard ships for export.

Today, Páfos is clearly divided into three parts, beginning with *Káto Páfos* down on the sea with its fishing port. The extensive hotel district has grown up north and east of the harbour. The chain of hotels now stretches along the beach to Geroskípou.

Today, most local residents live in the upper town of *Ktíma,* built during the Turkish era on a plateau some 2–3km (1¼–1¾mi) inland. Here, you'll find mostly shops, schools and government offices; at the seaside, souvenir shops, restaurants and bars rule the roost.

And finally there's *Palaiá Páfos,* the site of the ancient town which, in 321 BC, was abandoned in favour of the newly found-

Tombs of the Kings – without kings

ed *Néa Páfos*, which today consists of the Ktíma and Káto Páfos parts of town. The rural village of *Koúklia* and a few fields of ruins from Antiquity now occupy the site where Palaiá Páfos once stood.

SIGHTSEEING

AGÍA SOLOMONÍ
In the Christian era, the rock tombs of the pagan world were put to various uses: as a prison, stone quarries or even chapels. This was also how the ancient rock tomb of Saint Solomoní was turned into a chapel. On the way down to the chapel you'll notice a conspicuous tree. Numerous kerchiefs and pieces of fabric have been knotted onto its branches. This ancient custom is deemed to make prayers said in the chapel more effective. *Apostolos Pavlos Avenue | free admission*

ARCHAEOLOGICAL PARK
The Archaeological Park shelters the mosaics, the Odeon and the Saranda Kolonnes fortress; all are described in detail below. You pay only once, at the ticket desk in the large car park at the port. Plan at least three hours for a proper look round. *June–Aug daily 8am–7.30pm, April/May and Sept/Oct daily 10am–7pm, Nov–March daily 10am–5pm | admission 4 euros*

ARCHAEOLOGICAL DISTRICT MUSEUM
This small museum boasts fine gold jewellery from the 15th century BC to the 3rd century AD, good examples of Roman glass and hot-water bottles made of clay representing limbs and other body parts. *Tue, Wed, Fri 8am–3pm, Thu 8am–5pm, Sat 9am–1pm | admission 2 euros | Dighénis Street*

BYZANTINE MUSEUM
Small collection of icons from the 12th–18th centuries, liturgical vestments and items. *June–Sept Mon–Fri 9am–4pm (Nov–March 9am–3pm), Sat 9am–1pm | admission 2 euros | Andréa Ioánnou Street | Ktíma*

HARBOUR *lovely!!*
The harbour jetty, which is only used for fishing and pleasure boats now, lies above one of the two older quays, of which a few stone blocks can still be seen at the far end. The Turkish fort at the start of the jetty is worth visiting for the

view across Páfos. *Fort June–Aug daily 8am–7.30pm, Nov–March daily 8am–5pm, at other times daily 8am–6pm | admission 2 euros*

ROYAL TOMBS

Of the residential houses of ancient Páfos nothing is left. The tombs however yield an idea of how wealthy Ptolemies lived in the last two centuries before the Christian era. The most beautiful were hewn out of the rocky soil near the sea and form a courtyard surrounded by columns or pillars. Several burial chambers radiate out from this courtyard. In one of those large tombs a massive rock was left standing in the courtyard, with a set of steps leading down to a well. Other parts of the complex were used as burial chambers. *June–Aug daily 8am–7.30pm, Nov–March daily 8am–5pm, at other times daily 8am–6pm | admission 2 euros | Tombs of the Kings Road*

MOSAICS

The centre of the Roman town used to lie to the northwest of the fishing port. The high walls that once surrounded it have not survived, but we know that spacious villas and administrative buildings decorated with precious floor mosaics once stood here. Since their discovery in 1962, a whole picture book of ancient mythology has been exposed and restored.

Most of the mosaics date from the 3rd and 4th centuries. They are spread across four different houses which the archaeologists named after the mosaics found inside.

A particularly beautiful mosaic in the ★ *House of Dionysos* is the large scene depicting the wine harvest full of vivid details.

The other mosaics also recount the myths of Antiquity in similarly graphic detail, full of drama and life. If you want to get to know them better, you are best off either taking part in a guided tour to the mosaics or buying an English guidebook at the ticket office.

From the House of Dionysos the trail continues to the *House of Aion,* with further representations of mythological themes. The next stop is the *House of Theseus* with an extraordinary mosaic, the centre of which is taken up by a large group of images around a representation of the Athenean hero Theseus, who has just vanquished the Minotaur in the maze on Crete. The personification of the maze is represented at the bottom left, the Minotaur down to the right in front of the hero. At the top right you'll see the island of Crete personified as a king; at the top left you can make out his daughter Ariadne, whose string allowed Theseus to find his way out of the labyrinth.

Finally, from the house of Theseus you reach the *House of Orpheus* with three more mosaics. *In the Archaeological Park*

★ **House of Dionysos**
Ancient mosaics telling stories full of drama and the zest for life
→ p. 67

★ **Baths of Aphrodite**
A calm spring pool in lush green surroundings with a touch of the erotic → p. 72

★ **Rocks of Aphrodite**
A charming stretch of coastline even without the legends
→ p. 72

★ **Ágios Neófytos Monastery**
800 year-old portraits of a hermit → p. 72

MARCO POLO HIGHLIGHTS

MUSEUM OF CYPRIOT CULTURAL LIFE

This private museum in a villa built in 1894 shows various well-presented objects from everyday Cypriot life over the past centuries. *Mon–Sat 10am–5.30pm, Sun 9am–1pm | admission 3 euros | Éxo Vrýssi Street 1*

ODEON 🔅

In the immediate vicinity of the mosaics, a short white lighthouse from the British era points skywards. Below the tower, the Roman Odeon has been exposed – a small theatre for lyrical contests and musical performances. From the twelve rows of seats you look down onto a large area which, in Antiquity, was pulsing with life – namely the Forum, the market place. *In the Archaeological Park*

ST PAUL'S COLUMN

The biblical Acts of the Apostles tell us that St Paul was in Páfos where he demonstrated the power of the Christian faith to the Roman proconsul, castigating a pagan sorcerer with blindness. Local legend also has it that St Paul was whipped here. The column that he was tied to while being whipped is on show on the site of an Early Christian basilica in medieval Panagía Chrissopolítissa Church.

SARANDA KOLONNES 🔅

One of the most heavily destroyed yet most beautiful of the ruined castles on Cyprus stands above the fishing port. The Crusaders built the castle straight after taking possession of the island in 1192. Razed by an earthquake only thirty years later it was then used as a quarry. Its name, meaning '40 columns', is due to the fact that 40 granite columns from the neighbouring Roman forum were reused in its construction. Some can be seen supporting the walls of the castle entrance to the east. *In the Archaeological Park*

FOOD & DRINK

INSIDER TIP LAÓNA 😊

Market pub serving dishes that are freshly prepared every day using local produce, including vegetarian dishes. Open in the evening twice a week for a small, large or a purely vegetarian *mesé* platter. *Mon–Sat 10am–4pm, Tue and Fri also 7pm–10pm | Vótsi Street 6 | Ktíma | Budget*

INSIDER TIP LATERNA 😊

Chrístos Mavromátis is proud of his vegetarian specialities and steaks from Cypriot cattle. In his small restaurant with an easy-going atmosphere this passionate cook offers a good selection of fine Cypriot wines from the region – amongst them organic wines by winemaker Ángelos Tsangarídi – at fair prices. *Daily from 5.30pm, closed in Dec | Apóllonos Street 2/corner Ágios Antónios Street | Káto Páfos | Moderate*

INSIDER TIP OTHOMANIC BATH TRADITIONAL COFFEE SHOP

Right in front of the former Turkish Baths, your hosts serve all kinds of sweets alongside salads and sandwiches, including the Cypriot rosewater speciality *mahalépi,* Oriental *baklavá* pastries with ice cream or Cypriot apple pie. Only soft Greek music can be heard through the speakers. *Daily 9am–6pm | betweenthe market hall and car park | Ktíma | tel. 99 45 25 48 | Budget*

SÓLI-AÉPIA 🔅

First-rate meat or fish mesé and panoramic views. Simple, good-value snacks served all day. *Odós Talaát Pása 1 | at the market hall | tel. 26 93 32 72 | live music Wed, Fri, Sat from 9pm | Moderate*

SHOPPING

MARKET HALL ●

As the market hall was taken over in the late 1990s by souvenir sellers, the many farmers who come here to sell their produce, mainly on a Saturday morning, have to make do with pitches around the hall. Still, the atmosphere has remained rural and authentic. *Mon, Tue, Thu, Fri 7.30am–4pm, Wed and Sat 7.30am–2pm | Agorás Street | Ktíma*

KÓSTAS THEODÓROU

Leather goods made in Cyprus, mostly bags and accessories. *Makários Ave. 92 | Ktíma*

VAVOÚLAS

Exclusive shoe fashion for ladies and gentlemen, mainly by Greek footwear designers. *Níkos Nikolaídis Street 18 | Ktíma*

SPORTS & BEACHES

The town only has a few small man-made sandy beach areas in front of the hotels. The first larger beaches start at Geroskípou and below the old lighthouse at Odeon. The good sandy and pebbly beaches to the west of Páfos can be reached by bus.

Water sports are offered mostly by the large hotels; diving courses and excursions can also be arranged. Skipperless 40–150hp motorboats that only require a car drivers' license can be hired from *Chris Speed Boats* at the harbour *(tel. 99 69 90 41)*. The harbour is also the point of departure for deep-sea fishing tours *(tel. 99 42 10 44 | www.theangler-paphos.com)*. Boat trips to *Coral Bay* and *Lára Beach* leave from the harbour too. There is a golf course some 10km (6mi) out of town, southeast of the village of Tsáda. For guided walks in English in the surrounding countryside contact 😊 INSIDER TIP *Ecologia Tours (p. 106)*.

A convivial atmosphere rules where 2000 years ago pilgrims came ashore

Let your evenings become endless in the chic bars at the port of Pafós

BOOGIES KARAOKE CLUB
The courageous can of course grab the mike and go for it. The atmosphere resembles a casting show open to everybody. In the hotel district. *Daily 9pm–4.15am | Ágios Antónios Street/Bar Street*

DEMOKRITOS
Large pub with folkloristic programme and good *mesé*. In the hotel district. *Daily from 8pm | Ágios Antónios Street | Moderate*

RAINBOW
Cellar club with a long tradition – and air-conditioning. Music policy is mainly Garage and House. In the hotel district. *Daily from midnight | Ágios Antónios Street 1 | Moderate*

WHERE TO STAY

AGÍI ANÁRGYRI ● ☺ (134 B3) *(ᴥ B7)*
In the narrow green enchanted valley of Agíi Anárgyri, 19km (12mi) north of Pá-fos, a sulphurous well has been bubbling away for many years. Its healing water is now being used by the eponymous spa hotel, beautifully integrated into the landscape and built largely using natural materials. It also caters for day guests. Some of the hotel rooms even have mineral water on tap in the bathroom. *56 rooms | tel. 26 81 40 00 | www. aasparesort.com | Expensive*

ÁNEMI
Various studios and flats sleeping up to four, most of them furnished in a modern and tasteful style with well equipped kitchenettes in a central location in the hotel district east of the harbour, only a few minutes from the nightlife, numerous pubs and the harbour. Large pool, bar and restaurant. *80 flats | Kikerónos Street | tel. 26 94 56 66 | www.anemi hotelcyprus.com | Moderate–Expensive*

ANNABELLE
Luxury seaside hotel, only a stroll from the harbour. Small sandy beach, two pools. *198 rooms | Posidónos Street | tel.*

26 23 83 33 | *www.thanoshotels.com* |
Expensive

INSIDER**TIP** KINIRÁS

Kleánthis Gregoríou represents the fifth generation to run this romantic Old Town hotel founded back in 1922, and maintains the same tradition of hospitality as his father Geórgios who painted many of the pictures on the walls. The comfortable rooms are adorned with wall paintings by hotel guests. Cypriot specialities of the highest quality are served in the snug courtyard with palms, araucaria, medlar and other trees, not least an unsurpassed *stifádo. 18 rooms* | *Archbishop Makários Avenue 91* | *tel. 26 94 16 04* | *www.kiniras.cy.net* | *Moderate*

PÝRAMOS

Situated in the modern hotel district near the nightlife, yet quiet. *20 rooms* | *Ágios Anastasías Street 28* | *tel. 26 93 51 61* | *www.pyramos-hotel.com* | *Budget*

INFORMATION

CYPRUS TOURISM ORGANISATION

In the airport building | *open for all arrivals* | *tel. 26 00 73 68; Gladstone Street 3* | *Ktíma* | *tel. 26 93 28 41* and *Piátsa (opposite Hotel Annabelle)* | *tel. 26 93 05 21* | *Káto Páfos*

WHERE TO GO

ÁGIOS GEÓRGIOS (134 A4) (*Ø A7*)

Lying to the right of the road leading to this village, 19km (12mi) northwest, just past Coral Bay, the *Páfos Bird Park (April–Sep daily 9am–8pm, Oct–March daily 9am–5pm* | *admission 16 euros* | *www. pafosbirdpark.com) covers* 100,000 m². The ruined basilicas of Ágios Geórgios boast mosaics with representations of birds and turtles *(Mon–Sat 10am–4pm* |

admission 2 euros). 500m below the village, next to the sheltered fishing harbour, there is a small sandy beach with deckchairs for hire. The rocky coast is a popular place for walks.

INSIDER**TIP** ANÓGYRA (ANÓYIRA) (135 D5) (*Ø C8*)

Entering this very well maintained and flower-bedecked village 48km (30mi) east of Páfos, at an altitude of 470m (1540ft), you'll see, to the right of the road, the medieval church of *Ágios Ioánnis Theológos* with well-preserved monastic ruins *(freely accessible)*. The main sight, 3km (1¾mi) from the village, is the well-signposted olive oil press at ☺ *Oleástro*, where between November and February you can watch the production process. The olive oil made here is exclusively organic. There is also an olive oil museum with a large park, a small animal centre with pony rides for children, a good restaurant and a well-

LOW BUDGET

▶ Parking in Páfos: the car park in front of the Archaeological Park in Káto Páfos is free. The car park below the market hall of Ktíma will only set you back 1 euro/day.

▶ Guided tour for tight budgets: for just 5 euros you can explore the whole of Páfos and its surroundings by using the regular bus service. Bus no. 15 takes in the entire coast between Geroskípou and Coral Bay. From Coral Bay, bus no. 10 goes to the market hall, from where you can catch bus no. 10 or 11 back to the coastal hotels.

stocked souvenir shop *(daily 10am–7pm | admission 3 euros)*.

BATHS OF APHRODITE (LOUTRÁ TIS APHRODÍTIS) ★ (134 A2) *(⏷ A6)*

At the end of the short cobblestone path leading through a small, lush valley, you'll suddenly find yourself in front of a tiny spring-fed pond in a rocky cave. A fig tree provides shade, and ferns and flowers line the rocky shore. According to legend, this idyllic place – some 40km (25mi) north of Páfos – was the favourite bathing spot of the goddess Aphrodite. One day, the Athenian prince Akamás surprised her here, and a love story unfolded between the two which met with the disapproval of Zeus. The goddess of Love had to renounce earthly pleasures and return to the other Gods on Mount Olympus. *Freely accessible at all times*

CORAL BAY (134 A4) *(⏷ A8)*

On a peninsula between two completely built-up and always busy sandy beach coves 13km (8mi) above Páfos, archaeologists discovered traces of a Late Bronze Age settlement. Its most visible feature is the curtain wall, 3200 years old. *Mon–Sat 10am–4pm | admission 2 euros*

ROCKS OF APHRODITE ★ ☼ (134 D6) *(⏷ C9)*

There are several lonely pebbly beaches along this stretch of coastline with steep cliffs. Its western end, some 21km (13mi) southeast of Páfos, is marked by a small beach on this flatter part of the coast. Just off this beach several rocks just out of the sea. While their real name is 'Rocks of the Romeans', *Pétra tou Romioú*, the tourist board's publicity calls them the Rocks of Aphrodite, claiming that it was here that the goddess Aphrodite rose out of the waves.

GEROSKÍPOU (134 B5) *(⏷ B8)*

Along the main street you can pick up one of the village's specialities, *lukumia*, loukoumi, a fruit jelly-like sweet dusted with icing sugar and eaten like a praline. On the large village square the main sight of the village is the *Church of the Agía Paraskeví*. Its simple, seemingly ineptly built domes allow the church to be dated to the 9th or 10th century *(May–Oct daily 8am–1pm and 2pm–5pm, Nov–April daily 8am–1pm and 2pm–4pm | admission free)*. At the *folklore museum* near the church you can learn how silkworms were cultivated in Geroskípou up until World War II and silk produced *(daily 8.30am–4pm | admission 2 euros)*. *3km (2mi) east of Páfos*

ÁGIOS NEÓFYTOS MONASTERY ★ (134 B4) *(⏷ B8)*

On the slopes of the 613m (2011ft) Chárta mountain, 8km (5mi) north of Páfos at the end of a green valley, is one of the most beautiful monasteries in Cyprus. It is dedicated to a Cypriot saint who found-

It's at these rocks that Aphrodite is supposed to have risen from the sea – that's what the tourism brochures claim anyway

ed a hermitage here in 1159 which soon attracted many holy men. They lived in rock caves that they painted inside. Two of the paintings show the man himself, Neófytos, one standing between two angels, in another kneeling in front of the throne of Christ, flanked by Mary and John. The origins of today's monastery buildings reach back to the 15th century. *April–Oct daily 9am–1pm and 2pm–6pm, Nov–March daily 9am–1pm and 2pm–4pm | admission 85 cents*

PANAGÍA CHRYSORROGIÁTISSA MONASTERY ✲ (134 C4) (*C7*)

This 12th-century monastery lies high above a valley in the western foothills of the Tróodos mountains near the village of *Páno Panagiá, 35km (22mi)* northeast of Páfos. The church standing in the centre of the little monastic courtyard houses an icon of the Virgin Mary considered to work miracles. According to tradition it was painted by Luke the Evangelist. *Freely accessible at all times*

KOÚKLIA (PALAIÁ PÁFOS) (134 C6) (*B9*)

In Antiquity the most important Aphrodite sanctuary on Cyprus stood on a flat plateau above the coastal plain 15km (9mi) east of Páfos. It consisted of a closed courtyard where the goddess, in the form of a large dark stone, was revered. In Roman times a large courtyard was established at the entrance to the sanctuary surrounded by columned halls. The remains of some mosaics and foundation walls can still be seen. The *Château de Covocle* next to the excavations is now a *museum.* One of the exhibits on display here is a stone that might have been the sanctuary's cult object. The most impressive object is a INSIDER TIP sarcophagus from the Classical period discovered in 2007 bearing painted reliefs on all outer panels. They show a lion attacking a wild boar, a soldier carrying a wounded comrade and a scene of Odysseus and Diomedes fighting. Unique anywhere in the world is the scene where Odysseus and three of his

At Latsí harbour, a small fleet ensures the fish restaurants of Pólis are never caught short

companions cling on to the underside of a ram to escape the giant Polyphem. In its current appearance, the manor dates from the Turkish era. A Gothic hall however points to the fact that, in Frankish times, the sugarcane plantations of the kings were administered from here. *Fri–Wed 9am–4pm, Thu 8am–5pm | admission 3.40 euros*

INSIDER TIP **LÉMBA** (134 B5) (*∅ A8*)
Painters, sculptors and potters work in Lémba, 6km (4mi) north of Páfos. Near the road leading from Lémba to the sea, you can visit an excavated Bronze Age settlement over 4500 years old and the reconstruction of the village. *Freely accessible*

PÁNO PANAGIÁ (PANAYIÁ) (135 D4) (*∅ C7*)
This winegrowers' village at an altitude of 800m, some 37km (23mi) northeast of Páfos, was the birthplace of Archbishop Makários. A small *museum (daily 9am–1pm and 2pm–4pm | admission approx. 50 cents)* on the square with his

monument serves as a reminder of his life's work. This is also where you can pick up the key to the humble house where he was born.

PÓLIS (134 B2) (*∅ B6*)
Of all the larger holiday resorts in southern Cyprus, Pólis is the most rural. To get there, drive 35km (22mi) north of Páfos. Small apartment houses and hotels nestling between a lot of greenery dominate the picture. The largest hotel in the area, well integrated into the landscape, is also the most luxurious and expensive on all of Cyprus: the *Anássa (183 rooms | Néo Chorió | tel. 26 88 80 00 | www.thanoshotels. com | Expensive)*. A good-value complex of holiday flights in the heart of this little town is the freindly *Hotel Mariéla (64 rooms | Arsinoe Street 3 | tel. 26 33 23 09 | www.mariela-hotel. com | Budget)*. At Pólis the beach reaches from the eucalyptus forest at the campsite to the fishing port of Latsí with the excellent fish tavern *Yiángos & Peter* right on the quay *(daily from*

9am | *Moderate*). The best restaurant is the *Archontaríki* (daily from 12.30pm | *Moderate*). The *Archaeological Museum (Markaríou Street 26 | Tue, Wed, Fri 8am–3pm, Thu 8am–5pm, Sat 9am–3pm | admission 2 euros)* includes finds from the ancient town of Márion on the same site. The nightlife is concentrated around the town's pedestrian precinct, just 250m long, with its café bars and restaurants. A good place to meet people for a chat is the pub *Costas Corner*. The proprietors speak excellent English (daily from 10am | *Gríva Digéni Street 6 | Budget*). The relatively flat surrounding area is well suited for cycling tours and the range of water sports on offer is good too.

STAVRÓS TIS PSÓKAS ●
(135 D2) (*ᴔ C6*)

Amidst the lonely forest scenery of the western Tróodos range, 41mk (25½mi) from Páfos in the north, is the state-run forest administration. The coffee-house serves as both restaurant and grocery store. In the shady barbecue area immediately below, anyone who has remembered to bring charcoal and meat can stage a hearty picnic. There is an enclosure too with a few wild sheep.

CEDAR VALLEY (135 D3) (*ᴔ C6–7*)

In Antiquity, Cyprus was covered in cedar forests. The trees later fell victim to shipbuilding and construction, as well as charcoal production. It was the British who in the 1930s began the task of reforestation, so that there are now over 30,000 specimens, most of them of a good size. For the best view of the cedars across the valley, follow the way-marked ⛷ hiking trail a few miles east of Stavrós tis Psókas leading up the 1362m (4468ft)-high Mount Tripilos, for around 30 minutes.

BOOKS & FILMS

▶ **The Emperor Awakes** – historical pageturner (2011) by Alexis Konnaris set partly on Cyprus. Escapism and history lesson in one. Also available for Kindle

▶ **Bitter Lemons** – a classic suffused with poetry and humour. The British novelist Lawrence Durrell recounts his life on Cyprus from the 1950s

▶ **Face of an Island:** 24 short stories from Cyprus – selection of short stories in English edited by Panos Ioannides, available, for example, through *www. hellenicbookservice.com*

▶ **Exodus** – the novel by Leon Uris is not only the great epos about the foundation of the state of Israel. It is partly set on Cyprus and was filmed by Otto Preminger starring Paul Newman in the lead role (1960)

▶ **DVD Cities of the World** – A 60-minute commercial travelogue produced in 2009

▶ **Cyprus** – The Moment Time Stood Still – a 1995, six-part, real-life drama series about Greek-Cypriot traumas in the wake of 1974, set in Nicosia

TRÓODOS

It is in the many villages in the Tróodos mountains that you'll find the authentic Cyprus at its best. Stroll down alleyways, many of them decked out in flowers, chat to the locals in cosy basic coffeehouses on village squares. The food and the taverns are rural and rustic, and in the many small guesthouses and hotels guests are still looked after properly.

Something completely unique here are the barn-roofed churches which now enjoy Unesco World Heritage status. The guardians who hold the keys will open up these little sanctuaries especially for you. You'll come across Orthodox piety in monasteries, far removed from the cares of world. Yet even the most remote regions are connected by good if bendy roads leading through vineyards and forests. There are many waymarked hiking trails to get a better look at the natural scenery. Wineries are open for visits – and the views are usually sublime. Many peaks afford views all the way to the sea and far across the Mesaória; on this plain's other side, the Kerýneia Mountains flank the northern coast. Maybe you'll be lucky and see some griffon vultures high up in the sky. On a hot summer's day, you'll certainly appreciate the pleasantly fresh air at an altitude of up to 2000m (6500ft).

The people in the Tróodos area only derive a small part of their living from tourism. When they're not working in coastal towns and commuting there and back every day, they usually live from wine production, fruit farming and livestock

Photo: Kýkko Monastery

Mountains and monasteries: the mountainous area around Ólympos, the island's highest peak, is full of picturesque surprises

breeding. Mining – mainly chromium and asbestos – which up to a few years ago played an important role in the Tróodos area, has however now ceased.

WHERE TO GO

INSIDER TIP ▶ AGÍA MÁVRA
(135 F4) (*m* D8)

To find the tallest plane trees on all Cyprus head for a narrow gorge on the minor road leading from *Péra Pédi* to *Koiláni*. Here the small church of *Agía Mávra*

has been watching over a bubbling well since the 15th century. Inside you'll find a few 17th century frescoes. The faithful have made numerous votive offerings of wax: replicas of babies or adults and of individual body parts.

AGRÓS (136 B2) (*m* E7)

This large village in the east of the Tróodos region lies on a slope at an altitude of 1000m (3280ft) in a wide elevated valley. In May, countless roses bloom here and rosewater is extracted from

At over 600m (1900ft), Galáta has always been a refuge for city folk plagued by the heat

their petals. The *Tsolákis Distillery (signposted on the main street at the hospital | open for visits and shopping daily sunrise to sunset | www.rose-tsolakis.com)* also produces rose liqueur and wine, rose cosmetics and perfume. The *Kafkália butchers* on the main road produces *lúndsa*, a Cypriot variation of salted pork chops, the *pastúrma* cured beef and smoked pork sausages all year round. To the right, in an unnamed factory above the connecting road between the main road and the rose water distillery, you can watch seasonal fruit and vegetables being marinated in sugar syrup to make desserts and sweet teatime treats.

GALÁTA (135 F3) (*Ø E6*)

Galáta is situated in the Solea Valley on the northern slope of the Tróodos mountains at some 600m (1960ft), between fruit trees and slim poplar trees. In medieval times, Venetian and Byzantine noblemen used to enjoy coming here on a hot summer's day. Today, Galáta is one of the villages city dwellers visit in the evening and at weekends to escape from the heat in Nicosia. Amongst the 19th-century houses in the village, the restored caravanserai of *Hani Kalliana* can be found right on the through road. Galáta also boasts four Byzantine barn-roofed churches, of which two are definitely worth a visit for their wall paintings and photogenic surroundings: *Panagía Podíthu* and *Archángelos.* Ask for the keys to the churches in the large coffeehouse on the platía.

Panagía Podíthu was built in 1502 as the church for a monastery that has since vanished without trace. Its fresco ornamentation reveals the influence of the Italian Renaissance. The patron for these paintings was a Frankish officer who obviously chose an artist who painted according to his tastes.

The much smaller *Church of the Archangels* (Archángeli, 1514), only a few yards away, has wall paintings in a rustic style not at all influenced by the Renaissance, even though here too the patron was a Frankish nobleman. The patron is represented with his family below a depiction of Christ Enthroned.

KAKOPETRIÁ ★ (135 F3) *(◇ E7)*

The modern village, whose name translates as 'Bad Rock', is Galáta's immediate neighbour, directly above, and is even more in demand as a cooler retreat for the summer. The listed historical core of the village was built on a long extended slab of rock between two small riverbeds in a narrow valley at an altitude of about 700m (2300ft). You're best off wandering along the main street, where mostly elderly ladies sell herbs and other natural products from the island, take a seat for a few minutes on the balcony of the small *Kafenío Serenity* (*Budget*) on the tiny village square or in the *Pandóchio Línos* tavern and bar (*Moderate*), ancient houses where the tranquillity of the old village is the most perceptible. The watermill next to the conspicuous Mílos/Mill hotel is also worth seeing.

5km (3mi) outside Kakopetriá you can discover a jewel of Byzantine art: the *Ágios Nikólaos tis Stégis* church dating back to the 11th century (*Tue–Sat 9am–4pm, Sun 11am–4pm | free admission*). Dating from different centuries and illustrating various styles, its wall paintings are considered medieval masterpieces.

KALOPANAGIÓTIS (135 E3) *(◇ D7)*

Built on a steep slope, this village lies some 750m (2460ft) above sea level in the lower Marathássa valley above a small reservoir lake. If you're coming from Pedoulás, you'll see to the left of the main street as you enter the village a INSIDER TIP *dschudschúko* production plant where the sweet speciality you'll find for sale all over the island at markets and on street stalls is produced all year round. Almonds or walnuts are strung up on three-pronged branches. Dipped several times over into boiling grape must, they are then hung up to dry, very photogenically, on the terrace.

The historical sight here is the *Ágios Giánnis Lampadistís monastery* (*Mon–Sat 8am–noon and 1.30pm–5pm | free admission*) in the little valley below the village. The monastery boasts valuable frescoes mainly dating to the 13th and 15th centuries. The former monastic cells are now attractiveyl used to display old agricultural equipment such as an oil and a wine press. Immediately behind the monastery, a modern museum presents valuable icons from the monastery.

★ **Kakopetriá**
Listed village between two babbling brooks → p. 79

★ **Kýkko Monastery**
Immeasurable riches to this day – thanks to an icon of the Virgin Mary → p. 80

★ **Ómodos**
Picture-postcard mountain village with pretty platía → p. 82

★ **Tróodos**
Experience nature on foot → p. 83

MARCO POLO HIGHLIGHTS

KÝKKO MONASTERY ★

(135 D3) (*ळ D7*)

The most famous monastery on Cyprus, Kýkko, occupies a solitary position far from any village at an altitude of 1140m (3740ft) on the slopes of a ridge of the same name. Its austere exterior conceals two courtyards with light arcades and magnificent mosaics on a golden background, the church – the entire interior of which was painted around 1995 – and a very modern *museum,* designed with the splendour of a palace and containing art treasures of immeasurable value. All parts of the monastic complex, rebuilt following a fire in 1813, are very well looked after.

The most important cult object in the monastery is an icon of the Virgin Mary said to have been painted by Luke the Evangelist on a panel, given to him by an archangel for the purpose. This icon, today hanging on the iconostasis and covered with silver and gold, has reputedly worked many miracles. In particular it is said to have brought long-awaited rain to entire parched regions. To give thanks for this, the monastery received gifts time and again. It accumulated a considerable wealth and today own hotels and industrial facilities, as well as a lot of other property on Cyprus. Attached to the monastery are hotel-like lodgings for pilgrims, numerous souvenir stalls leased from the monastery, as well as a restaurant. If you'd rather entrust your wishes to nature than to an icon, feel free to attach them to a ● *wishing tree* in the monastery.

Kýkko is not only a religious but also a national, historical pilgrimage site for Greek Cypriots. It was near the monastery that General Grivas, the leader of the struggle for independence against the British, pitched his headquarters. The monks did a lot to support him. In fact, one of their number, Archbishop Makários, became the spiritual leader of the liberation movement and is buried near the monastery. A well-maintained tarmac road leads up to Mount Throní just over a mile away, where soldiers keep a guard of honour at his grave. The small chapel near Makários' tomb has a modern mosaic icon of the Mother of God of Kýkko. *Monastery and grave accessible in daytime | free admission (monastery museum 3 euros)*

TROODÍTISSA MONASTERY

(135 E4) (*ळ D7*)

In contrast to Kýkko, the Troodítissa monastery seems very humble. Instead of business and politics its monks devote themselves to growing apples and raising cattle. In the monastery church of 1731, look out for an icon of the Virgin Mother with embossed silver. It is a place of pilgrimage for many women who have been wishing for a child for some

LOW BUDGET

▶ Pick your own: a free holiday experience with a difference is on offer at the Tsolákis Distillery in Agrós (*p. 78*) in May and early June. Volunteers are invited to pick the flowers needed for the distillation of rose water – between 4am–9am. Register under: *tel. 25 52 18 93*

▶ Picnic everywhere: Cyprus has several hundred official picnic sites set up by the forest administration. There is a surfeit of them in the Tróodos Mountains and they usually have drinking water available, as well as a barbecue.

On Mount Ólympos: no Gods anywhere, but fabulous views

time. *Please note that non-Orthodox visitors are not allowed in the monastery*

KOILÁNI (135 E3) (*ﾑ D8*)

Up until 1974, Koiláni was a village inhabited by both Muslims and Christians, as evidenced by the small mosque in the immediate vicinity of the church. The village has several wineries that may be visited during the daytime.

LAGOUDERÁ (136 B1–2) (*ﾑ E7*)

On the edge of this tranquil mountain village in the eastern Tróodos you'll find the particularly beautiful church of *Panagía tu Aráku*. During the Crusades, the domed edifice built in the late 12th century received additional protection in the shape of a barn roof so typical for the Tróodos region; this one here nearly reaches the ground. Created around 1200 by a master from Constantinople, the frescoes inside are impressive thanks to the dignity and expressive qualities of its figures.

The key to the church is held by the village priest, who can either be found in the former monastery wing next to the church or in a coffeehouse. *Free admission, but purchase of a postcard or two is expected*

ÓLYMPOS (135 E–F3) (*ﾑ D7*)

At 1951m (6400ft), the highest elevation on Cyprus, Mount Ólympos can often be seen from many parts of the island, as the white radar domes of the British military and the Cypriot television transmitter masts mark its double peak. Because of this use the entire summit area has been out of bounds to civilians since 1999. While the signposts leading the way to the summit are still there, it's only worth following them in the winter to reach the ski lifts and runs on the slope of Mount Olympus.

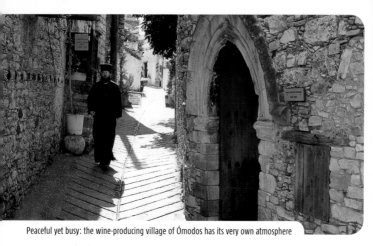

Peaceful yet busy: the wine-producing village of Ómodos has its very own atmosphere

ÓMODOS ⭐ (135 E4) (*D8*)

The winegrowing village on the mountain slope opposite Páno Plátres is particularly atmospheric. Flanked by a number of cafés, the large cobblestoned platía has got to be one of the most beautiful village squares on Cyprus. Ómodos is also a good place to do your souvenir shopping. Have a look at the glass shop in the alleyway leading to the wine press! The heart of Ómodos is the no longer inhabited *Stavrós Monastery* at the lower end of the platía. The monastery church preserves the relic of the skull of the Apostle Philip, as well as a splinter from the Cross and remains of the ropes used to tie Christ to the Cross.

If you leave the monastery by the northern door, you'll reach the main lane, leading past souvenir shops and traditionally furnished houses that are open to visitors, to the *Línos* medieval wine press *(open in the daytime | free admission)*. You can taste and buy wine in another time-honoured vaulted building next to it. The *Olympus* winery on the edge of the village is also open to visitors *(Mon–Fri 10am–4pm)*.

PÁNO PLÁTRES (135 E4) (*D7*)

With its many hotels and taverns, this small town at 1100m (3600ft), is a popular destination for visitors looking to escape the summer heat and is the centre of tourism in the Tróodos mountains. There are lots of visitors in the peak of summer and during the skiing season in January and February and, while there are no sights as such, Páno Plátres is a good base for making trips to other parts of the mountains.

INSIDER TIP ▸ PÁNO PÝRGOS
(135 D1) (*C5*)

If you take a drive from Kýkko Monastery to the northern coast, it's worth making a detour to this exceedingly remote village whose inhabitants still operate dozens of charcoal stacks in the surrounding area. If you explore the area a bit, you'll come across the various stages of charcoal production at close range.

PEDOULÁS (135 E3) (*D7*)

The village near Mount Olympus is the centre of Cypriot cherry cultivation. The small barn-roofed church of *Ágios Michaíl* near the main church, visible from afar, has rustic wall paintings dating from 1474. To see medieval and post-Byzantine icons, head for the *Icons Museum* in the Classicist building of the former village school opposite *(April–Oct daily 9.30am–1pm and 2pm–6pm, Nov–March daily 9.30am–1pm and 2pm–5pm | free admission).*

PHÍNI (FOÍNI) (135 E4) *(Ⓜ D7)*

For a long time, this large mountain village was one of the centres of the pottery industry on Cyprus. Today, there are only two small ceramics workshops still operating. Definitely worth seeing is the private *Pivlákion Folk Museum* with an important collection of ceramics *(signposted on village road | if closed enquire at nearest coffeehouse | admission 1.50 euros).*

STAVRÓS TOU AGIASMÁTI
(136 B1) *(Ⓜ E7)*

Amidst the forested mountains of the eastern Tróodos, you'll find the lonely barn-roofed church of *Stavrós tou Agiasmáti.* If you can track down the holder of the key in one of the coffeehouses in the village of Platanistássa, 4km (2½mi) away, you can also see the ornamental frescoes inside. Note the 15th-century paintings in a wall niche in the left-hand church wall. They show Emperor Constantine's conversion to Christianity and the discovery of the True Cross of Christ by the Emperor's mother Helena. The custodian can also show you the start of a 3–4 hour hiking trail, marked with red dots, mainly through the forest to the village of Lagouderá *(p. 81).*

TRÓODOS ★ (135 F3–4) *(Ⓜ D7)*

At an altitude of over 1700m (5500ft), a small holiday resort has been established just below Mount Ólympos. Several pubs, a hotel, campsite, riding stables with horses for hire, and tennis courts are available. The *Tróodos Visitors Centre (daily 10am–4pm | admission 1 euro)* shows a 10-minute video on the flora and geology of the mountains; the adjoining 250m educational trail will introduce you to the local plants and rock formations. In winter you can hire skis on the way from Tróodos onto Mount Ólympos. Tróodos is the starting point of a well-waymarked nature trail that, at an altitude of 1700m (a good 5500ft), follows a virtually level course almost right round Mount Olympus, and tells you about he plants and geology and offers plenty of beautiful vistas. The trail is 12km (7½mi) long and joins the Pródromos-Tróodos road, along which you can walk back the remaining 4km (2½mi). The hike is not taxing and can be easily done in trainers.

CYPRUS' WILDLIFE

The only larger mammal living in the Tróodos forests today is the Cypriot wild sheep, the mouflon. Apart from on stamps, however, you'll at best see it in the enclosure at *Stavrós tis Psókas.* The numerous flamingos to be seen in winter in the salt lakes of Lárnaka and Ak-rotíri are the most conspicuous form of wildlife on the island. In the mountains you'll occasionally spot black vultures, hawks, long-legged buzzards, peregrine falcons, kestrels and Eleonora's falcons. You're unlikely to see any snakes.

VOUNÍ (135 E5) (*ω D8*)

This large and very photogenic mountain village boasts a particularly uniform appearance due to the large number of old buildings. The entire village in fact is listed. Combine traditional rural living and excellent Cypriot food in the old village house of INSIDERTIP *I Lófou* (6 rooms | tel. 25 47 02 02 | www.cyprus-living.co.uk | Budget) with its pretty courtyard.

FOOD & DRINK

While you'll find many restaurants in Kakopetriá, Páno Plátres and Tróodos, you can also eat at Kýkko Monastery, in Ómodos and Pedoulás, Pródromos and Agrós. There are further eateries along the main roads leading through the mountains.

AGÍA MÁVRI (135 E4) (*ω D8*)

At weekends and in the month of August, this modern restaurant opposite the Agía Mávri chapel near Koiláni is popular with locals who come here to enjoy the generous *mesé* and the XXL pork chops. *Daily from noon | along the road between Péra Pedí and Koiláni | Moderate*

INSIDERTIP BYZÁNTIO (135 E3) (*ω D7*)

Every lunchtime the tavern at the roundabout of the highest village on Cyprus sets up a large and tasty buffet of specialities (13 euros). *Daily from 11am | Pródromos | Budget*

HARRY'S SPRING WATER (135 E3) (*ω D7*)

This old and very basic tavern on a side road between Pródromos and Pedoulás is a destination for the especially courageous. Apart from all the usual dishes, they serve (at least at weekends) grilled lambs' heads, lamb liver and salted goat's meat called *tsamarélla*. *Daily from noon | Pedoulás | Budget*

MÍLOS/MILL ⚜ (135 F3) (*ω E7*)

The restaurant on the upper floor of the architecturally interesting *Mill Hotel* is among the best on Cyprus. Making a reservation is advisable. Particularly delicious is the INSIDERTIP salmon trout (deboned first, if you ask!) with an olive oil/lemon-garlic sauce. *Daily from noon | Kakopetriá | tel. 22 92 25 36 | www.cymillhotel.com | Moderate*

SAINT ANTONIO (135 E4) (*ω D7*)

Sunday lunch buffet, *mesé* in the evening – the Cypriot and international à la carte

---

AN ICON AS A PATRON

Like so many monastic foundations on Cyprus, the one at Troodítissa is also said to go back to a miraculous order given by an icon. Hermits, who had found an image of the Virgin Mary 1000 years ago in a cave, started building a chapel for the icon on the site of their find. However, every morning, the work they had done the day before, would always have collapsed and the icon disappeared several times. It was always found again by the men on the same spot, as well at the site of today's monastery. This at last made it clear to them where Mary wanted her church built. The miracle attracted other holy men, resulting in the foundation of the monastic community.

dishes and homemade cakes are always tasty. *Daily from 10am | Makários Street 3 | Páno Plátres | Moderate*

the only sound comes from a babbling brook. *Kakopetriá | tel. 22 92 31 61 | www. linos-inn.com.cy | Moderate–Expensive*

Home of fine mocha and easy-going serenity: traditional coffeehouses like this one in Vouní

WHERE TO STAY

FOREST PARK (135 E4) (*M D7*)
Best hotel in the mountains, with a very English atmosphere! There's a pool under the trees as well as an indoor pool. Make sure you ask for a room in the new building! *137 rooms | Páno Plátres | tel. 25 42 17 51 | www.forestparkhotel.com.cy | Expensive*

JUBILEE (135 F3) (*M D7*)
Hotel 1757m (5764ft) above sea level overlooking the village of Tróodos on the Ólympos road. While retro lovers appreciate the simple colonial atmosphere, some visitors will not appreciate the lack of mod cons in the bathroom. *37 rooms | tel. 25 42 01 07 | www.jubileehotel.com | Moderate*

INSIDER TIP PANDOCHÍON LÍNOS (135 F3) (*M E7*)
22 traditionally furnished rooms, some of them with a jacuzzi, in natural stone houses in the listed part of the village. You won't have to worry about cars and mopeds keeping you awake at night here,

PENDELI (135 E4) (*M D7*)
Well-equipped, centrally-located hotel with a pool. *81 rooms | Páno Plátres | tel. 25 42 17 36 | www.cyprushotelsonline.net/ pendelihotelplatres.htm | Expensive*

PETIT PALAIS (135 E4) (*M D7*)
Modern, four-storey hotel in the centre. The ☀ rooms on the two top floors have a good view of the mountains. Pretty café terrace. *32 rooms | Páno Plátres | tel. 25 42 27 23 | www.petitpalaishotel.com | Budget–Moderate*

RODON (136 B2) (*M E7*)
Modern hotel with pool in an exposed position high above the village. In peak summer season the hotel management organises guided walks and other activities so you can get to know the region. *155 rooms | Agrós | tel. 25 52 12 01 | http:// rodonhotel.com | Moderate*

INFORMATION

CYPRUS TOURISM ORGANISATION
On village square in Páno Plátres | tel. 25 42 13 16

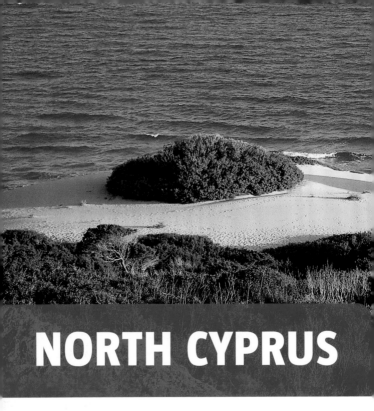

NORTH CYPRUS

The northern part of the island is at least as beautiful as the south. However, between July 1974 and May 2004 you were only able to visit it on short day trips from southern Cyprus.

At the time, travellers who really really wanted to spend their holiday in northern Cyprus had to face a tedious journey lasting at least seven hours, including a stop in Turkey. This all changed with the admission of southern Cyprus to the EU in May 2004. Now anybody can spend their holiday anywhere on Cyprus. However, the Greek Cypriots still demand that you enter via southern Cyprus using Lárnaka or Páfos airports.

The landscape of northern Cyprus is dominated by the Kerýneia mountains stretching along the northern coast up to 1000m (3280ft) above sea level, which have an alpine character in many places, dramatic rock precipices and bizarre knolls. On the Karpaz Peninsula the scenery changes to softer hills enclosing small fertile valleys. In the far west, northern Cyprus also claims part of the foothills of the Tróodos mountains – and nearly half of the extensive Mesaória plain, in the centre of the island, belongs to the north.

Apart from northern Nicosia, Kerýneia and Famagusta are the only towns in northern Cyprus. Otherwise the northern part of the island is mainly rural. However, since 2004 there has been a lot of construction work. Huge urban conglomerations, often of shocking monotony, have already sprawled from Lapta to

Photo: Golden Beach near Dipkarpaz

A Sleeping Beauty awakening: for a long time, tourism in northern Cyprus lagged far behind the south. But there's so much to discover here

Esentepe along the northern coast, and from Famagusta to beyond Bogaz on the eastern coast. These stretches also contain nearly all the tourist hotels in northern Cyprus. The Karpaz Peninsula however, has remained unspoilt, offering only a few and usually fairly basic hotels.

FAMAGUSTA

(139 E2) (*M L5–6*) **Famagusta (Greek: Ammóchostos, pop. 30,000) was the most important port on the island – until 1974. Nearly all the hotels on Cyprus used to be concentrated here.**

In medieval times, Famagusta was the most important city on the island, ahead of Nicosia even, and in the 14th century boasted more than 70,000 inhabitants. It was via its port that trade with Asia Minor and northern Africa was carried out, bringing Famagusta enormous wealth. Its noble inhabitants were very rich and founded numerous large churches whose ruins are still standing today. They form a charming contrast to the partly but prettily restored Old Town and the minarets that some Christian churches acquired following their conversion into mosques.

SIGHTSEEING

ÁGIOS GEÓRGIOS CHURCH

The former Orthodox cathedral of Famagusta was built in the 15th century, its external appearance being in the splendidly majestic Gothic style. Immediately adjoining its southern wall is a smaller church in the typical Byzantine style, where the emphasis is more on the decoration of the interior. *Freely accessible | M. Ersu Sok.*

LALA MUSTAFA MOSQUE ⭐

A good 90 years after work was started on the Gothic cathedral of Nicosia and shortly after the expulsion of the last Crusaders from the Holy Land, the Frankish kingdom on Cyprus prospered to the extent that of a second cathedral was begun in Famagusta, completed in only 28 years and consecrated at the same time as St Sophia in Nicosia, in 1326. Built in the Gothic style, its magnificent western façade is reminiscent of the Gothic cathedrals of France. Only an attached minaret reveals that the church was turned into a mosque in 1571. On the left-hand side in front of the mosque are a sycamore and a ● mulberry fig tree, said to be as old as the building. And in the shade you can watch the comings and goings in front of the church. *Freely accessible*

The Lala Mustafa Mosque was consecrated in 1326 – as a Gothic cathedral

LAND GATE & CITY WALLS

This imposing gate forms part of the city fortifications completed by the Venetians in 1565 and which you can see well from the bastion. The thickness of the 4km (over 2mi)-long city wall reaches 7m, and up to 18m in height. The Turkish name for the Land Gate is *Akkule* ('White Tower'), as it was here that the Venetians raised their first white flag in 1571 as a sign of their capitulation.

OTHELLO TOWER ☆

In medieval times, the port of Famagusta was secured by a citadel integrated in the city walls. Since the British colonial period it has been called Othello Tower, as Shakespeare's tragedy is set on Cyprus, and this small castle is the best candidate for the murder of Othello's spouse Desdemona. *May–Sept daily 9am–7pm, Oct–April daily 9am–1pm and 2pm–4.45pm | admission 7 YTL | Cengiz Topel*

PALAZZO DEL PROVVEDITORE

Today, the tall ruins of the Venetian governor's palace enclose a small park with a simple café. Opposite the café a set of steps leads up to the *Namik Kemal Museum* honouring a Turkish poet born in 1840 and held here for four years for his verses that incited rebellion *(open in the daytime | free admission)*.

VARÓSHA ●

Once the tourist centre of the island up until 1974, Varósha is now a ghost town, as the Greek-Cypriot population in this part of town had to flee. High rises riddled with bullet holes are flanked by construction cranes erected back in 1974; in the supermarkets the groceries have been gaining mould for over 35 years. Apart from a Turkish officer's casino there is not a single inhabited building in Varósha, which is cut off from the rest of Famagusta by a barbed-wire fence. The best vantage point to survey this sad vista is from the beach in front of Palm Beach hotel.

FOOD & DRINK

INSIDER TIP ▶ CYPRUS HOUSE
Excellent regional cuisine in the atmosphere of a 1930s village house. Pretty garden with the capitals of columns from Antiquity. *Daily noon–1pm | Polat Pasha Bulvarı | tel. 3 66 48 45 | Moderate*

D & B

The most modern restaurant in the Old Town. Pizza, pasta, salads, steaks, kebabs. *Daily from 10am | Namek Kemal Maydani 14 | Budget*

★ Lala Mustafa Mosque
Famagusta's main mosque was originally built as a Christian cathedral → p. 88

★ Golden Beach
Plenty of beach and golden sand, devoid of people → p. 91

★ Sálamis
An ancient city with a large amphitheatre and extensive burial grounds → p. 92

★ Kerýneia harbour
Fish taverns, boats and a castle set against a bizarre mountain backdrop → p. 94

★ Bellapaís/Beylerbeyi
Gothic abbey on the green slopes of the Kerýneia mountains → p. 95

★ St Hilárion
Crusader castle with a sea view → p. 97

MARCO POLO HIGHLIGHTS

GINKGO

Chic restaurant with modern furnishings in a colonial building next to the cathedral. Food selection of soups too. *Daily from 11am | Liman Yolu 1 | Budget–Moderate*

PETEK PASTANESI

The best pastry place in the Old Town, selling small snacks and Turkish cakes. *Daily 9am–8pm | Yesil Deniz Sok. 1 | Budget*

SPORTS & BEACHES

The ● beach at Palm Beach Hotel is freely accessible. However, for a good swim you're better off heading out to the long – and also free – ● sandy beach in front of the excavations of Sálamis, where water sports are also available.

ENTERTAINMENT

With the help of the EU, a hip district has sprung up in *Palace Street,* beginning at the Lala Mustafa Mosque, with lounges and bars in old market halls and warehouses.

WHERE TO STAY

PALM BEACH

Only first-class hotel in town, right on the beach and bordering Varósha. Large pool, disco, water sports facilities. *108 rooms | Deve Limani | tel. 3 66 20 00 | www.north ernpalmbeach.com | Expensive*

PORTOFINO

Modern hotel in the New Town. Large air-conditioned rooms; the roof has a ☆ bar restaurant with views of the Old Town. *52 rooms | Fevzi Çakmak Bulvarı 9 | tel. 3 66 43 92 | www.porto finohotel-cyprus.com | Budget*

INFORMATION

GAZIMAGUSA TURIZM

Fevzi Çakmak Bulvarı | tel. 3 66 28 64

WHERE TO GO

ÁGIOS FÝLON/APHENDRÍKA
(133 E2) (*ᗡ* O2)

Only 4km (2½mi) north of Dipkarpaz/ Rizokárpaso, a good 89km (55mi) from Famagusta, right by the sea, the cross-domed church of *Ágios Phyllon* was built in the 11th century on the foundations of a basilica. The fish served in the simple ● tavern *Oasis at Ayfilon (tel. 0 53 38 68 55 91 | www.oasishotelkarpas. com | Budget)* is always fresh. They also have six basic rooms right by the water. Stretching 300m to the west is a 600m-long beach of fine sand, completely devoid of shade, which winds itself around a bay like a sickle. You'll find more good sandy beaches near the track leading 7km (4mi) to the ancient town of Aphendríka which includes the ruins of three churches.

DIPKARPAZ (RIZOKÁRPASO)
(133 D2) (*ᗡ* O2)

In the main town on the Karpaz Peninsula, Turkish and Greek Cypriots still live together. There is an Orthodox priest and a Greek primary and middle school. The houses in the village are scattered far and wide across a green valley between low hills. To catch the special atmosphere of this place, just spend a little while in the Greek coffeehouse *(closed 1pm–5pm)*. A good place to stay is on the upper edge of the village in *Karpaz Arch Houses (12 units | tel. 3 72 20 09 | www. karpazarchhouses.com | Budget)*. You'll find an excellent choice for your dinner right next door at INSIDER TIP *Restaurant Manolyam (daily from 6pm | Budget)*.

Imposing Crusader castle with splendid views: from Kantára you can see all the way to Famagusta

ENKOMI-ALASIA (139 D2) (🕮 L5)

This Bronze Age settlement 8km (5mi) northwest of Famagusta near Tuzla/Enkomi was inhabited for nearly a millennium between 2000 and 1075 BC. Enkomi was a centre of copper smelting. The famous 'Horned God' now in the Cyprus Museum in Nicosia was found here. The only things to see in situ are the right-angled street layout as well as the foundation walls of sanctuaries, houses and a palace. *May–Sept daily 8am–7pm, Oct–April daily 8am–1pm and 2.30pm–5pm | admission 5 YTL*

GOLDEN BEACH ★ (133 E2) (🕮 P2)

Golden Beach lies a good 97km (60mi) from Famagusta nearly on the eastern tip of the Karpaz Peninsula. 3km (nearly 2mi)-long and several hundred metres wide, its edge is marked by high dunes, in part covered in sparse vegetation. Outside the months of July and August is it more or less deserted, but even in the height of summer there is still a lot of space for the *Caretta caretta* marine turtles that lay their eggs here. The extensive beach area only has four tavernas

which in peak season open around the clock. The nearest hotel with a bit more comfort lies 15km (9mi) in the direction of Dipkarpaz: the *Blue Sea (12 rooms | tel. 3 72 23 93 | Moderate)*. The owner also takes guests out to fish with him.

INSIDER TIP KANTÁRA ☼

(133 E4) (🕮 L3)

At an altitude of 630m (2060ft), the former Crusader castle on the eastern edge of the Kerýneia mountains affords splendid views of the Karpaz Peninsula to the east and the bay of Famagusta to the south. On a clear day you can even see Mount Stavrovoúni near Lárnaka. *May–Sept daily 10am–5pm, Oct–April daily 9am–1pm and 2.30pm–6.45pm | admission 5 YTL*

APÓSTOLOS ANDRÉAS MONASTERY

(133 F1) (🕮 P1)

Since 23 April, 2003 – the day when Greek Cypriots were allowed to enter northern Cyprus for the first time since 1974 – the monastery at the tip of the Karpaz Peninsula, which has become shockingly run-down on the outside, has

Headless, but impressively ancient: in the palestra of Sálamis

become an important pilgrimage site for Cypriot Christians. It was here that the Apostle Andréas worked a miracle during one of his ship journeys in the 1st century AD. The drinking water aboard had run out and the captain had turned blind. The Apostle ordered the crew to hit the sword against a rock – and lo and behold a well began to gush water. During a later trip the captain was to leave an icon with the image of the Apostle on this site, which became the origin of a monastery. Today's church dates from 1867. Especially at weekends, numerous street vendors wait outside the monastery offering cheap souvenirs, costume jewellery and nuts. *Freely accessible*

BARNABÁS MONASTERY (MONÍ APÓSTOLOU VARNÁVA)
(139 D2) (*Ø L5*)

Legend has it that the Apostle Barnabas, who accompanied St Paul on his missionary journey through Cyprus, was murdered in Sálamis. Today, a small modern chapel stands above the grave of the Apostle, some 100m below Barnabás Monastery, probably founded in the 5th century 8km (5mi) north of Famagusta. Originally built in the 10th century, that church was remodelled in the 18th century. Today, the monastery holds a small *Archaeological Museum*. The large monastery church includes a number of icons. *May–Sept daily 9am–7pm, Oct–April daily 8am–5.30pm | admission 7 YTL incl. Tombs of the Kings*

SÁLAMIS ★ (139 E2) (*Ø L5*)

The best overview of the extent of ancient Sálamis north of Famagusta is gained from the upper rungs of the Roman amphitheatre, which held 15,000 spectators. No less impressive are the columns and floors of the Roman/Early Christian palestra (training area for wrestlers and sportsmen), including a well-preserved ancient communal latrine for 44 people. The excavation area also includes the walls of two Early Christian basilicas and an ancient temple dedicated to Zeus. Outside the fenced-in town area left of the road leading to Barnabás Monastery, you'll see some strange earthen mounds. They mark the ancient necropolis, whose graves, in contrast to the ruins of the town, don't date from the Roman era but as far back as the 7th and 6th centuries BC. *May–Sept daily 9am–7pm, Oct–April daily 9am–4.45pm | admission excavations 9 YTL, tombs 7 YTL incl. Barnabás Monastery*

YENIERENKÖY (AIGIÁLOUSA)
(132 B3) *(Ⓜ N2)*

The large inland town which, up until 1974 was the centre of the Cypriot tobacco industry, has excellent sandy beaches in its vicinity reached from the road to Dipkarpaz. From Famagusta to here it's 60km (37mi). *Halk Plaj* and *Malibu Beach* near the town caters to all tourist needs. Still completely undiscovered is the belt of dunes 7km (4mi) east of Ágios Thýrsos. INSIDER TIP *Hotel Balci Plaza* not far from here is currently the best hotel on the Karpaz Peninsula *(12 rooms | tel. 0 53 38 62 93 03 | Skype: balciplaza | www.balciplaza.com | Moderate)*.

KERÝNEIA/ GIRNE

(131 D–E2) *(Ⓜ G4)* **Only 24km (15mi) – some 25 minutes by car – from Nicosia, beyond the narrow chain of the Kerýneia mountains, lies the most beautiful town on Cyprus (pop. 8000). Its Turkish name today is Girne.**

Its centre is formed by the small nearly circular harbour basin dating back to the Venetian period. The shore is lined by cafés and restaurants, sheltering centuries-old houses. One side of the port is occupied by an imposing fort. Within the Old Town a church tower and a minaret soar above the houses. Immediately beyond the town, the land rises steeply towards the mountains. The alpine-like summits of the Pendedáktilos are an intoxicating sight. The narrow plain along the northern coast supports many lemon and orange trees.

The ruins of a Gothic abbey can be found on the slope of the mountains in the village of Bellapaís, close to Kerýneia. A detour from the road leading to Nicosia takes day-trippers to the Crusader castle of Saint Hilárion.

SIGHTSEEING

CASTLE ☼
The castle that dominates the harbour, was erected in the Byzantine era and

LOW BUDGET

▶ The taverns on Golden Beach rent out very basic beach huts too, which will set you back about 70 YTL/night. Best bring your own sleeping bag. *Big Sand | tel. 0 53 38 65 34 88, Hasan's Turtle Beach | tel. 0 53 38 64 10 63, Burhan's Place | tel. 0 53 38 64 10 63 | www. burhansgoldenbeach.com*

▶ A good place in Kerýneia/Girne to stock up on things is the market on the edge of the Old Town, such as in the *Café de Paris* where an *Adana kebab* costs only 12 YTL.

extended and adapted according to the military and technical advances of the day by the Franks and the Venetians. Its walls afford the most fabulous view across Kerýneia and the mountains. *May–Sept daily 9am–8pm, Oct–April daily 9am–4.45pm | admission 12.50 YTL*

HARBOUR ⭐
Byzantine and Venetian ships already appreciated the pretty harbour of Kerýneia. Right in the centre of the entrance to the harbour you can make out a ruined tower from which, in medieval times, a chain could be spanned across to what is today the Customs House, as a form of protection from unwanted guests.

SHIPWRECK MUSEUM
2300 years ago a merchant vessel sank off the coast of Kerýneia. Its wreck and cargo have since been brought up from the seabed by archaeologists. The ship was over 4m wide and over 14m long. Its cargo reveals the route of its last journey. The 400 wine amphorae are from Samos und Kos. The ship also had 29 stone cereal mills and 9000 almonds which can still be identified as such today. The finds can now be admired in the castle museum. *May–Sept daily 9am–8pm, Oct–April daily 9am–4.45pm | admission included in the ticket to the castle*

FOOD & DRINK

If you've only got one day in Kerýneia, the most atmospheric places for food can be found at the harbour, though there are numerous taverns in the town and in the neighbouring bays.

BRASSERIE
This fancy restaurant run by a British-Italian couple is housed in an old colonial-style villa with a terrace opposite the Old Town mosque. *Daily noon–3pm and from 7pm | Efeler Sok. 2 | Expensive*

O PSARÁS ÁPO TO ZYGÍ/CANLI BALIK
A Turkish Cypriot, who before 1974 used to be a fisherman in the southern Cyp-

View across the fort on the pretty harbour of Kerýneia

riot town of Zygí, today runs the fish restaurant at the harbour, whose Greek name translates as 'The fisherman from Zygí'. The fish served here is guaranteed to have come straight off the boat onto your plate. *Daily 11am–midnight | harbour promenade | Moderate*

SPORTS & BEACHES

There are no beaches in Kerýneia, only facilities to allow you to enter the sea from the rocky coast. To swim, take your hire car, the bus or a taxi to neighbouring bays: *Acapulco Beach* (10km/6mi east), *Lara Beach* (28/17½mi east) or *Deniz Kizi Beach* (8km/5mi west).

A fine day at sea with several opportunities for swimming can be had on a day trip from the harbour aboard a wooden motorsailer; the ● Barbarossa was inspired by a pirate vessel, a so-called *gület* (approx. 48 YLT).

ENTERTAINMENT

The 13 casinos offer gambling, shows and other entertainment. Several hotels have in-house clubs, amongst them the Hotel *Dome* right by the sea. The most atmospheric pub in the Old Town is the *Horseshoe Bar (daily from 7pm | Canbulat Sok.)*.

WHERE TO STAY

Hotels can be found not only in the city but also in the small villages on the slopes of the Kerýneia mountains and along the coast, especially towards the west.

INSIDER TIP ▶ COURTYARD INN

Hotel complex with a lot of greenery and a small pool in the courtyard, just over a mile east of the city centre. Choose between four air-conditioned hotel rooms

and four bungalows with kitchenettes. The restaurant with sociable bar serves Cypriot, European and Indo-Pakistani food. *Karakórum/Karakum | on the Kerýneia-Bellapaís road | tel. 8 15 33 43 | www. courtyard-inn-cyprus.com | Budget*

DOME

The luxury hotel from the 1930s offers an updated version of classical refined charm, a ☀ rock terrace with pool right by the sea, as well as a casino and club. *160 rooms | Kordon Boyu | tel. 8 25 24 53 | www.domehotelcyprus.com | Moderate*

INSIDER TIP ▶ WHITE PEARL ☀

The only hotel right on the harbour offers a panoramic harbour view from seven out of its ten rooms. Friendly, familiar atmosphere, roof garden café. *Eftal Akca Sokaki 23 | tel. 8 15 04 29 | www. whitepearlhotel.com | Moderate*

INFORMATION

GIRNE MARINA TURIZM OFISI
At the harbour | tel. 8 15 21 45

WHERE TO GO

BESPARMAK (PENDADÁKTYLOS)
(131 F2–3) (*∅ H4*)
The main road from Kerýneia to Famagusta leads past the very distinctive 740m (2427ft)-high 'Five-Finger Mountain'. On the top of the pass, a surprise awaits: the INSIDER TIP ▶ *Besparmak-Buffavento* tavern *(daily from 9am | Budget)* built entirely of wood. The inviting interior has tastefully folkloristic furnishings und serves excellent kebab and kléftiko.

BELLAPAÍS/BEYLERBEYI ★
(131 E2) (*∅ G4*)
The pretty mountain village south of Kerýneia, inhabited by Greek Cypriots

before 1974, can boast the most romantic ruins in the country. Augustine monks founded an abbey here in 1205. The magnificent lancet arches of the former cloisters, the large still intact refectory and the cellars in the Gothic style are evidence of the wealth the abbey quickly acquired. A visit lasts 30 mins. *(summer daily 9am–8pm, winter daily 9am–4.45pm | admission 9 YTL)*. While the food is rather average, a fuel stop at the ⚲ *Restaurant Kybele (daily from 10am | Moderate)* is worth it for the intoxicating view. A good accommodation option at the upper edge of the village in bungalows set amongst a lush garden with pool terrace is the *Ambélia Tourist Village (60 rooms | tel. 8 15 36 55 | www. cyprus-ambelia.com | Budget)*.

GEMIKONAĞI (SÓLI) (135 E1) (*Ø D5*)
53km (33mi) southwest of Kerýneia, this is the site of a ruined amphitheatre and an Early Christian basilica belonging to the town founded by settlers from Athens around 600 BC. Until the 4th century, copper mining was Sóli's main source of income. The mosaic floor of the basilica includes exquisite depictions of animals *(May–Sept daily 9am–7pm, Oct–April daily 9am–4.45pm | admission 7 YTL)*.

On the coast road, modern *Soli Inn (23 rooms | tel. 7 27 73 41 | Budget)* with a pool is suitable for an overnight stay by the seaside. An excellent place for food on the coast is INSIDER TIP *Mardin (daily from 10am | Budget)* 50 m east of the excavations.

GÜZELYURT (MORFOU)
(130 B4) (*Ø E5*)
This small town amidst orange groves, 40 (25mi) southwest of Kerýneia, is a rural settlement with little of interest apart from the *Archaeological Museum,* featuring a statue of the multi-breasted goddess Artemis from Roman times *(May–Sept daily 9am–6.30pm, Oct–April daily 9am–4.30pm | admission 7 YTL)*, and the neighbouring 18th-century *Ágios Mámas* church with a sarcophagus said to contain the remains of an Early Christian Cypriot saint *(key held at museum)*.

INSIDER TIP LEFKE (LÉFKA)
(135 E1) (*Ø D6*)
This small university town nearly completely overlooked by tourism occupies a particularly beautiful position in the foothills of the Tróodos mountains between lush green and tall date palms – 55km (34mi) southwest of Kerýneia.

DAZZLING DIVERSITY

Like all places on Cyprus the northern Cypriot towns and villages also have a Greek name. Many of them had Turkish names even before 1974 and, since 1974, they all have one. Famagusta is the Venetian-English name for a city that is called Ammóchostos in Greek and Gazimağusa in Turkish. Greek-Cypriot island maps usually only give the Greek place names, the Turkish-Cypriot maps only the Turkish. This MARCO POLO guidebook gives both. While you'll usually only find the Turkish names on signs and signposts, in the wake of the new freedom of movement now occasionally the additional Greek names have started to appear again.

Here you'll still find a good number of traditional Turkish houses with their typical wooden bay windows. One of them has been converted into the atmospheric *Hotel Lefke Gardens (21 rooms | tel. 728 82 23 | www.lefkegardenshotel. com | Budget)*.

INSIDERTIP ▶ KARAMAN (KÁRMI)
(131 D2) (∅ G4)

This village 10km (6 mi) southwest of Kerýneia, entirely Greek-Cypriot up un-

ST HILÁRION ★ ☆
(131 D2) (∅ G4)

On a clear day, the view from the peaks of the Kerýneia mountains reaches all the way to the Turkish coast. Which is why the Byzantines built fortified castles on some of them to keep an eye on the sea between Cyprus and Asia Minor. The biggest and best-preserved of them is Ágios Hilárion Castle south of Kerýneia. *March–Sept daily 9am–6pm, Oct–April daily 9am–4.30pm | admission 7 YTL*

Only the best will do: in Karaman, foreign owners have restored many old houses

til 1974, is today mainly inhabited by foreigners who have preserved the old Greek houses in an exemplary fashion. There's even a red phonebox from colonial days standing next to the church. In the evenings and at weekends, small restaurants and bars attract outside visitors from afar and there are holiday homes for rent in the virtually car-free village too *(http://www.holidaylettings.co.uk/karaman-karmi)*.

VOÚNI (135 E1) (∅ D5)

In 1928/29 archaeologists uncovered the remains of a palace inhabited between about 500 and 380 BC on the ☆ plateau at the top of an 255m (836ft)-high hill, 35km (22mi) southwest of Kerýneia. 140 rooms and a thermal bath complex once extended over three levels. It is not known who resided here. *May–Sept daily 10am–5pm, Oct–April daily 9am–4.45pm | admission 5 YTL*

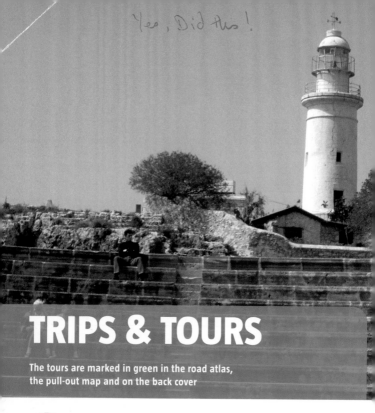

Yes, Did this!

TRIPS & TOURS

The tours are marked in green in the road atlas,
the pull-out map and on the back cover

1 ONE DAY IN THE TRÓODOS MOUNTAINS

The sheer variety on Cyprus reveals itself to those who spend at least one day in the mountains. Discover quiet towns, pretty villages, beautiful valleys, unique churches and monasteries and enjoy the aromatic forest air. Length of round trip from/to Limassol: approx. 175km (108mi). Time required: roughly 10–12 hours.

Start off by taking motorway exit no. 28 near Limassol, heading into the mountains on the good country road. Follow signs to Plátres. Pass the two **reservoirs** of **Polemídia Dam** and **Koúris Dam**, where you may fish but not swim. The main beneficiaries of the water supply from both reservoirs are the extensive plantations west of Limassol. The two villages of Monágri to the left and Lánia to the right of the main road are worth a detour. **Monágri**'s main attraction is its particularly fine church. In contrast, **Laniá** is a quiet village with many carefully restored traditional houses, some of them occupied by artists and craftspeople who live and work there.

Carry on along the main road towards Mount Ólympos, which you can see clearly from afar. Just beyond the village of **Trimiklíni**, the road forks. First continue in the direction of Nicosia, then take a left at the top of the pass towards Tróodos, passing the huge **open-cast mining area** where, up until the 1980s, asbestos was mined. While

Photo: In the Archaeological Park of Páfos

Discover a different part of Cyprus every day: today the home of Aphrodite, tomorrow Mount Olympus, and the day after Golden Beach

the gigantic area on a slope is today very slowly being reforested, it will remain a wound marring the pretty landscape for a long time to come. You can still see sections of asbestos-bearing rock right by the side of the road – dark chunks of rock criss-crossed by light bands of asbestos.

The bendy road now leads further uphill through sparse forest past various picnic areas. The most characteristic plants for the area are the holm oak, black pine and strawberry tree. Holm oaks look

different from their western and central European counterparts: you only really recognise them when you stop and find acorns below the trees. Older black pines are easily identified by the fact that their heavy branches bow down with dignity. Strawberry trees have distinct red, very smooth and seemingly barkless trunks.

At 1700m (5577ft) you reach the hamlet of Tróodos → p. 83. Here you can enjoy a coffee or tea in the refreshingly cool mountain air, but also stock up at several open-air stalls with marching provisions: pecan and walnuts from the Tróodos mountains as well as regional dry fruit.

The next part on the programme is driving once around the whole of Mount Ólympos. For this, first head to the village of Pródromos → p. 84, famous for its apples, and from there on to the spa resort of Páno Plátres → p. 82. Here, sweet-toothed travellers will enjoy a visit to the small **chocolate factory** right on the village road. While the cocoa mass is imported from Belgium, the varied fillings of the pralinés are the owners' own creations.

A good place to sit down for a rest is the winegrowing village of Ómodos → p. 82. Following a visit to the local monastery and a stroll through the romantic narrow streets, a coffee on the prettiest village square on the island is a particular treat. Tasteful souvenirs can also be found here.

The return trip to Ómodos on the coast is another sublime experience through breathtaking scenery as you drive down through INSIDER TIP the valley of the Diarízos. Right at the start you'll pass the large village of Ágios Nikólaos, whose mosque is evidence of its Turkish-Cypriot settlement history up to 1974. Up to that point, the ancestors of today's inhabitants had lived in the area of Mórphou/Güzelyürt in today's northern Cyprus, cultivating oranges. For life in the area they sought refuge, they had to be retrained to be winegrowers.

The valley shelters several former Turkish-Cypriot villages which have either been abandoned or are only inhabited by one farming family and their animals, with large sheep and goat herds roaming the green slopes. A good mile west of Koúklia → p. 73 you'll come to the old coastal road again.

2 HIKE AROUND MOUNT ÓLYMPOS

At an altitude of 1700m (5570ft) the ● ⚡ *Atalanta Trail,* an excellently waymarked, virtually flat nature trail leads once around the summit of the island's highest peak. Start and finish at the village of Tróodos where you can park your car. Length of the hike: 12km/7½mi. Don't forget to take water and provisions!

The Atalanta Trail is 1–3 m wide, well maintained and signed, with plenty of shade into the bargain. Benches have been placed at intervals along the path. The trail starts in the hamlet of Tróodos → p. 83 at the upper road junction. Your walk will be punctuated by continuously new vistas across the island. On a clear day you'll be able to make out the Akrotíri Peninsula and Limassol, Kýkko Monastery and Nicosia.

Particularly conspicuous trees along the route are the over 500-year old junipers and imposing black pines. The spring boasts lots of rockroses in full bloom. Their sticky leaves excrete the aromtic resin *labdanum* which used to be popular in the perfume industry. Farmers would harvest it herding goats through the plants, then shearing off their fetlocks and boiling the wool. Holm oaks are recognisable as such only by their acorns, not by the shape of their leaves. Occasionally you'll see a strawberry tree. In winter it bears edible fruit resembling strawberries.

After 7km (almost 4½mi), the trail passes the entrance to a mining shaft, in which chromium ore was mined until some 40 years ago. With the aid of a torch and at your own risk you can venture a few yards inside the shaft. After 8km (5mi), the trail reaches the tarmac road leading from Tróodos onto Mount

Easy hiking in the Tróodos Mountains: flat forest trails, plenty of shade and benches to relax on

Olympus. This is where you turn right and, after a few yards, you'll come across a signpost leading you onto a pretty forest trail. This one then ends near the starting point on the edge of Tróodos, where you can regain your strength in one of the cafés, the simple restaurants, or at farm stalls selling nuts and *dschudschúko,* a thickened and solidified grape must, which comes in the shape of long sausages.

3 THROUGH THE WEST OF THE ISLAND

The region around Páfos is considered the home of Aphrodite, the Goddess of Love. It is worth tracing her steps for a day by car. Length of the drive from the Rock of Aphrodite to Páfos: approx. 140km (87mi). Time required: at least 9–10 hours.

The starting point of your tour are the

Rocks of Aphrodite → p. 72. This is where the goddess from Antiquity is supposed to have risen from the sea and to have set foot on earth for the first time. From here, the old coastal road leads in a westerly direction through the wide, fertile, coastal plain of Páfos. After some ten minutes' drive you'll spot a small fortification, clearly visible above the slope of a low table mountain: **Covocle** marks the ancient Aphrodite sanctuary of **Palaiá Páfos** → p. 73. Take the old coastal road and continue to **Geroskípou** → p. 72. With its many sights, such as the Archaeological Park or the Tombs of the Kings, **Páfos** → p. 64 is worth a whole day of your holiday – so our tour just skirts the town on the way to **Pólis**. A worthwhile short detour beyond Páfos leads you to the monastery of **Ágios Neófytos** → p. 72 with its cave church painted all over inside. The main road first leads further up the slopes, initially still covered with many carob trees, later on changing to vineyards. Dipping down towards the northern coast, the road passes orange groves and tobacco fields, to eventually reach **Pólis** → p. 74. From here the drive leads through an enchanting coastal landscape to the **Baths of Aphrodite** → p. 72. For the drive back to the southern coast you can choose a shorter alternative route through villages that have still retained a fairly authentic character. **Droúseia** has cosy INSIDER**TIP** taverns and a small **Weavers' Museum,** exhibiting the silkworm cocoons *(Mon–Fri 8.30am–noon and 2pm–4pm, Sat 8.30am–noon | admission 50 cents | on the main road).* In the former basket weavers' village of **Iniá**, a small INSIDER**TIP** *museum* is dedicated to this craft *(signposted | daily 11am–6.30pm | free admission).*

Káthikas is worth a stop due to its good tavernas. When the first lights come on down below in Páfos, the drive from Káthikas via the large village of **Pégeia** is particularly impressive.

Remnants of a hermitage: splendid cave paintings in Ágios Neófytos Monastery

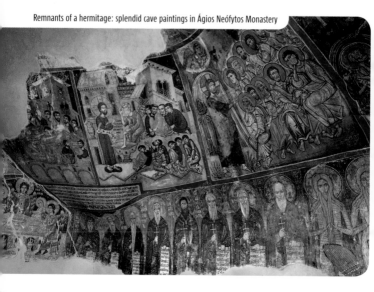

TRIPS & TOURS

4

HIKING NEAR AGÍA NÁPA

The best way to get close to the natural beauty of this small national park on Cape Gréko peninsula is to hike across it along small paths and wide trails, always with the sea in sight. The scheduled bus service takes you there cheaply from Agía Nápa and the region's other holiday resorts. Length of the hike: approx. 5km (3mi). Take water and provisions!

The near-treeless national park on the small peninsula between Agía Nápa and Paralímni-Protarás is an important habitat for migratory birds, as well as the site of many orchids and small Mediterranean flowering plants. From the bus stop on the main road, a tarmac road branches off towards the national park. Walk along it for about 600m and then follow the sign to the sea caves down 600m of unsurfaced track. Back on the small road stay on it until you reach the Agíi Anárgyri Chapel right by the sea, erected in 1922. Steps lead into the water. Just before you reach the chapel, on the right-hand side, is a photogenic rock arch just off the coast – the Kamára tou Koráka. From the chapel a short hiking trail leads to Kónnos Bay under a mile away. Take a dip and sample the refreshments at the small beach bar before walking to the main road (with bus stop) above the bay.

5

ON THE ROAD ON THE KARPAZ PENINSULA

This extended day trip takes in unique scenery, the most beautiful beach in all of northern Cyprus and a glimpse of life in those villages where Greek and Turkish Cypriots still live together. The length of the tour from/to Famagusta is approx. 240km (150mi), from/to Nicosia approx. 340km (210mi). Time required: from Famagusta at least 11, from Nicosia at least 13 hours.

East of Yeni Iskele/Trikomo, the roads coming from Nicosia and Famagusta meet. Drive along the coast to Bogázi (Bogaz), where you can take a break at the fishing port and go for a swim.

Beyond Ziyamet/Leonaríssou, turn right just before a petrol station towards Boltasli. At the entrance to the village, on the left-hand side, you'll see the well-preserved 12th-century Panagía Kanakária church which, however, can only be admired from outside. Driving through several rather shabby-looking villages, now lived in by Eastern Anatolians and Kurds, you'll pass wealthy Kaleburnu, where Turkish Cypriots have been living for centuries. An asphalt road takes you through small, very rural and lonely valleys to Dipkarpaz/Rizokárpaso → p. 90, the peninsula's main settlement.

It is here that the most beautiful part of the drive begins. Feral donkeys graze by the roadside, shepherds guide their flocks from one pasture to the next. Small roads lead down to the tavernas at Golden Beach → p. 91.

A few miles further on, the road leads to Apóstolos Andréas Monastery→ p. 91, the most important place of pilgrimage for Greek Cypriots. Less than another mile, the tarmac road ends at the Sea Bird restaurant (Budget) where, in summer, you can have a good lunch and even stay here too, albeit in very basic accommodation.

On the way back consider a detour from Dipkarpaz to the cross-domed church of Ágios Fýlon → p. 90. Carry on, past several beaches and small hotels to Yenierenköy/Aigiálousa → p. 93, where you can take a late dip in the sea before returning to Famagusta.

SPORTS & ACTIVITIES

Cyprus is the ideal choice for a sporty holiday. There is a wide range of options – and as the island is small and the roads well-maintained it is not difficult to sample a number of them.

CYCLING

A broad range of tours and training possibilities for both racing cyclists and mountainbikers starting from Limassol is available from the *bikeCyprus Center*, run *by* Thomas Wegmüller from Switzerland, with representatives in various hotels. Bikes only (without a tour) cannot be booked more than one or two weeks in advance. There is no permanent office *(tel. 25 63 40 93, mobile 99 66 62 00 | www.bikecyprus.com)*. Additional places to hire bikes are *Cyprus Villages Bike Center* in Tochní *(tel. 24 33 29 98 | www. cyprusvillages.com)* and *Aliathon Holiday Village Bike Center* in Páfos *(Poseidon Avenue | tel. 26 96 44 00 | www.aliathon village.com)*.

Several times a year mountainbike races are held, open to everyone. Information: *The Cyprus Cycling Federation (Amfipóleos Str. 21 | CY-2025 Stróvolos/Nicosia | tel. 22 44 98 70 | www.cypruscycling.com)*, which also organises non-commercial mountainbike tours which are mainly enjoyed by Cypriots.

In northern Cyprus, a private organisation is very active in the marking, GPS capture and description of mountainbike trails in the mountains and on the Karpaz Peninsula. For up-to-date information on

Swimming, riding, skiing: Cyprus is an outdoor mecca for sports fans. There is a huge variety of things to choose from

the current state of affairs see *www.kyre niamountaintrail.org*

DIVING

Diving schools and operators can be found in all beach resorts on Cyprus. Particularly appealing dives are on offer near Lárnaka, where the wreck of the 197m-long freighter Zenobia lies on the seabed. A decompression chamber is available at the hospital in Lárnaka and in the good *Dive-In* diving

school in Limassol *(Amathous Ave. 59 | tel. 25 311600 | www.dive-in.com.cy)*. The school has branches in Páfos und Lárnaka. Another recommended diving school is ● *Sunfish Divers* in Agía Nápa *(Makários Avenue 26 | tel. 23 721300 | www.sunfishdivers.com)*.

North Cyprus also has good diving schools, including the INSIDER TIP *Scuba Diving Center Amphora* founded in 1978 in Alsancak near Keryneia/Girne *(Yavuz Cikarma Plaji | tel. 8 514924 | www.am phoradiving.com)*.

GOLF

The golf courses on Cyprus are amongst the best in the Mediterranean. The *Mínthis Hills Golf Club*, 12km (7½mi) north of Páfos lies in a quiet, elevated valley and is possibly the only golf course in the world with a monastery that is still used in its grounds. Also in a valley, hunt down the *Secret Valley Golf Club* 17km (11mi) east of Páfos *(tel. for both 26 64 27 74 | www.cyprusgolf.com)*. On green hills near the Rock of Aphrodite, you can tee off at the *Aphrodite Hills Golf Course (tel. 26 82 82 00 | www.aphrodite-hills.com)*. Excellent rates are on offer at the *Vikla Country Club* near Kelláki *(tel. 99 67 42 18 | viklagolf@cytanet.com.cy)* 19 (12mi) from Limassol. Another golf course is being built in Tersefánou near Lárnaka.

The first golf course in northern Cyprus, the *Korineum Golf & Country Club (Esentepe | tel. 6 00 15 00 | www.korineumgolf. com)*, stretches across the slopes of the northern coast and the Kerýneia mountains, and has a classy club house, restaurant *(Budget)* and a shop. But don't thing that you can save money here compared to the south.

HEALTH CENTRES & SPAS

A visit to the old Ottoman *Omeriye Baths* → p. 57 in Nicosia, which were carefully restored and modernised in 2005, is an experiene not to be missed, providing perhaps the most atmospheric setting for relaxing and being pampered on the entire island. Chinese or aromatherapy massages cost 50 euros each, a 30-min. classic massage can be had for 30 euros, a 90-min. hot stones treatment is 80 euros *(couples Mon noon–9pm, men Tue, Thu, Sat 9am–9pm, women Wed, Fri, Sun 9am–9pm | admission with steam bath 20 euros | Tyrillías Square | southern Nicosia Old Town | tel. 22 46 05 70 | www. hamambaths.com)*.

HIKING

Most of the numerous well-marked hiking and nature trails can be found in the Tróodos mountains and on the Akamás Peninsula. They are often laid out as circular walks. Guided tours in the Tróodos mountains – particularly beautiful in spring – are run by the *Forest Park* Hotel in Páno Plátres for its guests → p. 85. In Páfos, you can join guided hikes which take a special look at environmental aspects; contact ⊙ INSIDER TIP *Ecologia Tours (Ágios Theódoros Street 2 | Ktíma | tel. 26 24 88 08 | http://www.cy-bay.com/ ecologia-tours.html)*.

PARAGLIDING

The only company on the island to offer tandem paragliding is *Highline Air Tours* in Kerýneia/Girne. A minibus will take you from your hotel to the starting point at an altitude of 750m (2460ft) near St Hilárion Castle. The landing point is right by the sea. The courageous glide back down to earth accompanied by an experienced pilot *(office at Kerýneia/ Girne harbour | tel. 54 28 55 56 72 | www. highlineparagliding.com | allow approx. 2 hrs)*.

RIDING

There are only a handful of professionally run stables offering hacks as well as lessons. One of them, near Kalavassós between Lárnaka and Limassol, is *Cyprus Villages & Traditional Houses Resort (tel. 24 33 29 98 | www.cyprus-villages.com)*. Near Limassol there is *Amathus Park Riding Club (tel. 99 60 41 09)*, and in Ágios

Geórgios near Páfos *George's Ranch (on the Coral Bay–Ágios Geórgios road | tel. 26 62 10 64)*.

Experienced riders should contact the *Çatalköy Riding Club* near Kerýneia/ Girne in northern Cyprus. The stables under British-Turkish management offer experiences ranging from an 80-minute trail around Bellapaís or a trailride to cosy pubs in the coastal plain all the way to challenging cross-country rides in the mountains and one-week programmes *(Çatalköy | tel. 8 45 47 41 | www.catalkoy ridingclub.com)*.

SAILING

As there are few marinas on Cyprus, the Greek islands are far away, and the Turkish ports may not be used from Cyprus for political reasons, charter options are limited here. *Information: Tourist Board Cyprus*

SKIING

Between Christmas and the end of February the slopes of Mount Olympus at altitudes of over 1700m (5570ft) often have enough snow for skiing. Four drag-lifts operate *(between 150 and 500m | day pass 23 euros)*. You can hire skis and shoes at the hut run by the *Cyprus Ski Club (16 euros/day, cross-country skis also available). Cyprus Ski Club | tel. 22 44 98 37 | www.cyprusski.com*

WINDSURFING

Opportunities for windsurfing and many other water sports are available at nearly all major beach hotels. Arguably the island's best windsurf and water sports centre is *West Water Sports* opposite the *Four Seasons Beach Hotel* in Limassol *(Amáthous Avenue | tel. 99 66 27 80 | www.westwatersports.com)*. Near Pólis: the *Latchi Watersports Centre (at the harbour | tel. 26 32 20 95 | www.latchi watersportscentre.com)*.

There are many exciting diving opportunities off the coast of Cyprus, both in the north and the south

TRAVEL WITH KIDS

Cyprus is an eminently child-friendly island. The Greeks' open and friendly nature is combined with a very British concern and care. Fabulous beaches and the Mediterranean are further guarantees for a holiday that even the youngest children will enjoy.

Nearly all hotel and restaurant owners have high chairs and car hire companies child seats. The range of baby food and nappies in supermarkets is as extensive as at home. In the evening children stay up into the small hours; Cypriots take the youngest members of the family with them when they go out for dinner, even if that involves staying out until well after midnight. Only a number of hotel bars don't allow children in the evening. While southern Cyprus has a range of special offers for families with children, they are still lacking in northern Cyprus.

AGÍA NÁPA & LÁRNAKA

CAMEL PARK (138 A6) (*∅ H8*)
Up until the World War II, camels were a fairly important means of transport on the island. Now they are back: at the camel park near Mazótos, and available for 15-minute rides. *Daily 9am–7pm (in winter until 5pm) | 30 min. ride 9 euros, children 6 euros | on the main road from Mazótos to Kíti | www.camel-park.com*

LUNA PARK (139 F4) (*∅ L–M7*)
While Agía Nápa is of course the club destination for adolescents, the younger

Fun in the water and on dry land: activities for the entire family, with the best reserved for the kids

kids can enjoy Luna Park – an entertainment park with merry-go-rounds, dodgems, an observation wheel and a kind of bungee-jumping tower called *Bungee Rocker. In summer daily from noon | in the centre of town on the minor road leading to Lárnaka*

WATERWORLD (139 E4) (*L7*)

After a session at the most beautiful and biggest water park on Cyprus on the edge of Agía Nápa, your kids will be pleasantly worn out. The action here is all focussed on the Trojan Horse. Water slides lead out of a replica of the famous mythological vehicle. Water pistols are available, and there's a large tub of water that will give the unguarded visitor a cold and wet surprise. The various giant slides in the park are up to 150m long, the wave machine creates waves of up to 1m high, and you can glide across Odysseus River in small round rubber dinghies. *April–Oct daily 10am–6pm | adults 32 euros, children (2–12 years) 18 euros, discount coupons (5/3 euros) available* on the homepage | Agía Thékla Road 18 | www.waterworldwaterpark.com

LIMASSOL

WATER MANIA (136 A5) (*ω E9*)

Limassol has its own watery fun park which is, however, a fair bit smaller than the one at Agía Nápa. Giant slides are the star attraction here. *Mid-April–mid-Oct daily 10am–5pm (peak summer season to 6pm) | adults 30 euros, children (3–12 years) 17 euros | Trachóni | shuttlebus service from hotels in Limassol and Páfos | tel. 25 71 42 35 | www.fasouri-watermania.com*

NICOSIA

TO TRENÁKI (U C5) (*ω c5*)

For younger children the divided island capital might not be a particularly attractive destination. One thing though they are certain to enjoy: a ride on the *trenáki,* the 'baby train' mini tram on rubber wheels starting daily every 20 minutes to a short round trip through Nicosia's Old Town. *Departures 10am–1pm and 3pm–7pm at the southern end of Lídras Steet | ticket 1.50 euros*

PÁFOS

APHRODITE WATERPARK (134 B5) (*ω A8*)

If your holiday base is Páfos, there's a water park here for when beach life has exhausted its attractions. Covering 35,000 m2, the extensive landscaped park is on the coast at Geroskípou and, like its bigger brothers in Agía Nápa and Limassol, also has giant slides. *Mid-April–Oct daily 10am–6pm | adults 29 euros, children (2–12 years) 16 euros | www.aphroditewaterpark.com*

DONKEY RIDES (134 B4) (*ω B7*)

Just before Káthikas on the road leading here from Páfos, *Trákkos Donkey Farm* awaits your custom. Trákkos has 80 donkeys available for rides. A one-hour ride costs 20 euros, with several riders allowed to take turns. *Tel. 99 64 70 31*

Always works and never gets boring: having fun at the Aphrodite Waterpark in Páfos

INSIDER TIP **KIVOTOS 3000**
(134 B2) (*∭ B6*)

Parents and children can expect a hearty welcome at the 'Ark 3000' café in Pólis. There is ice cream and hot waffles, board games and toys in the house and in the pretty garden, children's books as well as the owner's kids to play with. *July–Sept Mon–Sat 5pm–midnight, Tue–Sat also 11am–2pm, Oct–June Tue–Sat 11am–6pm | on the street leading from the village square to the police station | Budget*

VINTAGE BUS (134 B5) (*∭ A8*)

Until only a few years ago nearly every village had its own old-fashioned looking Bedford bus with the typical roofrack. One travel agency in Páfos acquired one of these old vehicles and uses it for excursions, that children will enjoy too, down unsurfaced roads and pitted tracks towards the Akamás Peninsula. English spoken. *Hercules Travel, at Páfos harbour | tel. 26 91 23 00 | day trips from 36 euros, children (2–12 years) 18 euros | www.hercules-travel.com*

TRÓODOS

DONKEY PARK (135 E4–5) (*∭ D8*)

The *Cyprus Donkey Sanctuary* is mainly run for the benefit of the animals, so while you can't feed the animals or ride them, you may look at them at your leisure and sponsor them. There is a souvenir shop and a small picnic area. Near the village of Vouní (where it is well signposted). *Daily 10am–4pm | free admission | sponsorship 20 euros/year | www.donkeysanctuarycyprus.org*

INSIDER TIP **HIKE ALONG THE WILD STREAM** (135 F4) (*∭ D7*)

One hike that is guaranteed to please even children who hate walking, is in the Tróodos mountains: over the course of 2½–3 hours, the *Caledonia Trail* leads downhill all the way along a pretty wild stream, which has to be crossed some 30 times on sometimes slightly wobbly stepping stones. Many a hiker has ended up with wet socks here. The valley is a jungle of green and the trail a rather narrow track. About halfway down you'll pass the most imposing waterfall on Cyprus, the *Caledonia Falls.* The hike is sure to be even more fun if you take some paper to make paper boats and watch how fast they travel.

At the end of the hike, take a refuelling stop at the *Psilo Dendro forest restaurant (Budget)*, where the freshly-caught trout is particularly good. The trail starts below the tarmac road leading from Páno Plátres (7km/3½mi) to Tróodos, where you'll find signs to the Caledonian Falls. There are no buses to the start; you'll have to take a taxi from Páno Plátres (approx. 8 euros) where the hike also finishes.

NORTH CYPRUS

BUBBLE MAKERS (132 B–C2) (*∭ N2*)

Special, two-hour, trial diving classes for children (that can already swim are run by the *Mephisto Diving* diving school from the Club Malibu Hotel on the Karpaz Peninsula. Following a thorough induction session, the little ones may descend with a mask and oxygen supply to depths of up to 2m (70 YTL). Adolescents may take part in day-long trial courses (165 YTL). *Erenköy Halk Plaji | tel. 53 38 67 37 74 | www.mephisto-diving.com*

FESTIVALS & EVENTS

There's a full calendar of events across the whole island. Tourist information offices in the south have up-to-date information in English so that you won't miss a thing.

FESTIVALS & EVENTS

GOOD FRIDAY

9pm: ▶ **processions** in all the towns and villages, particularly beautiful in Ktíma/Páfos

EASTER SATURDAY

11pm: ▶ **solemn religious services** in all churches, especially noteworthy in Ágios Neófytos Monastery in Páfos

EASTER SUNDAY

▶ *Fun Easter games* (e.g. sack and spoon races) in many towns and villages, especially in around Páfos

APRIL–JUNE

▶ ● *Musical Sundays.* Free concerts (folklore, jazz, classics, rock) in front of the Turkish fort in Páfos, at the *Onisilos Seaside Theatre* in Limassol and on the shore promenade of Lárnaka. Until mid-May starting at 11am, after that at 9pm

Religious, cultural or folkloric: there's always something going on somewhere on the island. You certainly won't get bored on Cyprus!

MAY/JUNE

▶ **INSIDER TIP** *International Bellapaís Music Festival.* Classical music events in the ruined monastery above Kerýneia/Girne. *www.bellapaisfestival.com*

JUNE

▶ *Shakespeare Festival.* Performances on several evenings in the ancient theatre of Koúrion

▶ *International Famagusta Art and Culture Festival* in the second half of the month. Theatre, dance and concerts in Sálamis and in front of the Othello Tower

THURSDAY BEFORE–TUESDAY AFTER WHITSUN

▶ *Feast of Kataklismós.* This festival in Lárnaka remembers Noah being saved from the Flood. The action is framed by a large fair on the sea promenade, concerts and sports events

15 AUGUST

▶ *Parish fairs* with music and dancing in many villages and at Kýkko Monastery

EARLY SEPTEMBER

▶ *Páfos Aphrodite Festival.* Three evenings of opera in front of the Turkish fort on Páfos harbour

1ST/2ND WEEKEND IN SEPTEMBER

▶ *Wine festival* in Limassol

13/14 SEPTEMBER

▶ *Parish fairs* in Ómodos, Páno Léfkara and at Stavrovoúni Monastery

SEPTEMBER/OCTOBER

▶ *Northern Cyprus Music Festival.* Classical, flamenco, rock and choral music in Kerýneia Castle, at Bellapaís Monastery and the Amphitheatre of Sálamis

3/4 OCTOBER

▶ *Parish fair* in Kalopanagiótis

LINKS, BLOGS, APPS & MORE

LINKS

▶ www.cypruswebsites.com Comprehensive metasite from Automobiles to Yachting

▶ www.cypruspictures.net Over 1300 pictures of various places and the scenery in southern Cyprus

▶ www.whatson-northcyprus.com Comprehensive website on northern Cyprus. Very useful: a well-maintained calendar of events on all northern Cypriot places of interest

▶ http://www.windowoncyprus.com/ Well-managed site with a food forum, free classified ads, pen friends and yacht crew lists

▶ www.kypros.org Find links to many institutions, but also monasteries and cultural organisations

▶ www.skicyprus.com Winter destination Cyprus: information and booking options for skiers and snowboarders

BLOGS & FORUMS

▶ www.cyprus-forum.com Large forum with plenty of useful information and issues on southern and northern Cyprus

▶ http://www.cyprus44.com/ Comprehensive updated travel information on North Cyprus. This site is also the communications forum for the English-speaking community

▶ http://www.expat-blog.com/en/destination/europe/cyprus/ Blogs by Cyprus-based Brits and other expats; useful information on the island and its people

▶ www.cyprusmeteo.com Apart from the current weather data on southern Cyprus you will find links to various beach and sea videos as well as some videos from Lárnaka

Regardless of whether you are still preparing your trip or already in Cyprus: these addresses will provide you with more information, videos and networks to make your holiday even more enjoyable

VIDEOS & STREAMS

▶ http://vimeo.com/14814095 Short commercial video on northern Cyprus

▶ http://vimeo.com/12390059 Underwater world off Lárnaka: 24-minute private video by Tony Parkinson of a dive down to the wreck of the 'Zenobia'

APPS

▶ AHIs OfflineCyprus Cypriot maps are uploaded to your smartphone, avoiding expensive roaming costs. You can save favourite places or add comments and photos

▶ Cyprus Guide Handy travel guide that works offline too. There is also a search function to find the contents of the individual categories, such as cashpoints, beaches, doctors, museums, nightlife or garages. An Internet connection is only required for sending virtual 'postcards' and to link to Facebook and Twitter

▶ Cyprus Mail This free app from the oldest newspaper on Cyprus, 'Cyprus Mail' provides up-to-date information in English on both parts of the island on a daily basis (except Mondays)

▶ WR Cyprus Radio This app gives you access to most Cypriot radio stations. You will need an Internet connection to use it

NETWORKS

▶ http://www.facebook.com/cyprusclubbing This Facebook-based blackboard of the English-speaking community receives up-to-date information and events notification on nightlife in southern Cyprus

▶ www.holidayphotosite.co.uk/Cyprus/cyprus_newmap.htm Picture gallery and a place to upload your holiday snaps

▶ http://twitter.com/cyprusevents Twitter blog run by Cyprusevents.net with up-to-date information on music and dance, theatre, cinema and art in southern Cyprus

The Publisher shall not be held responsible for the contents of the links, blogs, apps, etc. listed here

TRAVEL TIPS

ARRIVAL

✈ Travellers entering South Cyprus have two alternatives, i.e. two civilian airports: Lárnaka in the south and Páfos in the west of the island. And, in the opinion of the Greek-Cypriot government, only thxose arriving in Cyprus via those airports, or the seaport of Limassol, are entering the country legally. The airports of Lárnaka and Páfos are served by a number of airlines; flight time from England is approx. 4–5 hrs. The airport for North Cyprus is Ercan near Nicosia or, as an alternative, Gecitkale near Famagusta. Up until recently the only way to fly there was via Turkey, resulting in travel times of 7–10 hrs. Tickets on scheduled flights to Cyprus tend to be expensive, but Europe-based travellers may be able to pick up cheap, last-minute tickets with charter companies if they shop around. In practice, this applies only to travellers to the Republic of Cyprus, as charter tickets to Northern Cyprus are rarely available.

BANKS

Opening times in southern Cyprus: Mon–Fri 8.30am–noon, Northern Cyprus: 8am–noon, bank counters at the airports open for every arrival from abroad. In large cities and tourist centres, some banks in the south also open 4pm–6pm (May–Sept) or 3.30pm–5.30pm (Oct–April), in the north also 2pm–4pm (Oct–Apr). There are plenty of cashpoints all over Cyprus; in northern Cyprus they only dispense Turkish lira.

CAMPING

In northern Cyprus, camping is allowed anywhere. While prohibited in southern Cyprus, it is common in some areas. There are a number of campsites in both parts of the island.

RESPONSIBLE TRAVEL

It doesn't take a lot to be environmentally friendly whilst travelling. Don't just think about your carbon footprint whilst flying to and from your holiday destination but also about how you can protect nature and culture abroad. As a tourist it is especially important to respect nature, look out for local products, cycle instead of driving, save water and much more. If you would like to find out more about eco-tourism please visit: *www.ecotourism.org*

CAR HIRE

To hire a car, a national driving licence is sufficient. Depending on the season, a small car costs between 22 and 35 euros per day with unlimited mileage. Many car hire companies hand over the vehicle with a near-empty tank. If the tank is not completely empty or even full, the estimated content has to be paid for up front. Unused petrol is not refunded. Some hire companies in southern Cyprus also allow for their vehicles to be taken across the border into northern Cyprus. However, you'll have to take out a separate third-party insurance at the checkpoint (approx. 20 euros for 1–3 days, approx. 30 euros for 1 month).

From arrival to weather

Holiday from start to finish: the most important addresses and information for your trip to Cyprus

CONSULATES & EMBASSIES

BRITISH HIGH COMMISSION
Alexander Pallis Street (PO Box 21978) | 1587 Nicosia | tel. 357 22 861100 | www. ukincyprus.fco.gov.uk/en

EMBASSY OF THE REPUBLIC OF IRELAND
7, Aiantas Street (PO Box 23848) | Nicosia / tel. 357-22-818183 | e-mail: irishembassy @cytanet.com.cy

EMBASSY OF THE UNITED STATES OF AMERICA
Metochiou & Ploutarchou Street | 2407, Engomi | Nicosia | tel. 357 22 393939 | http://cyprus.usembassy.gov/index.html

EMBASSY OF CANADA (GREECE)
4, Ioannou Gennadiou Street / 115 21 Athens / Greece / tel. 30-210-7273400 / e-mail: athns@international.gc.ca

DRIVING

Cyprus drives on the left. Drivers coming from the right have the right of way. The speed limit within built-up ar-

BUDGETING

Taxi	0.50 £ / 0.8 $ per km (day/night)
Mocha	1.65 £ / 2.60 $ a cup
Deckchair	5 £ / 8 $ a day for two
Wine	from 8 £ / 13 $ for a bottle in a restaurant
Petrol	approx. 1 £ / 1.65 $ for 1 litre (super unleaded)
Kebab	3.30 £ / 5.30 $ for one portion in pita bread

eas is 50km/h (30mph), on rural roads 80km/h (50mph), in northern Cyprus 100 km/h (62mph), on motorways 100 km/h (62mph). The permitted blood alcohol level is 0.5; in northern Cyprus 0.0! Wearing a seatbelt on both front and back seats is mandatory. Children under 5 are not allowed to occupy a front seat. Using mobile phones and smoking while driving are prohibited.

CUSTOMS

EU citizens may import and export goods for personal use duty-free (e.g. 800 cigarettes or 1 kg tobacco, 90 l wine or 10 l spirits). North American citizens are subject to much tighter restrictions (1 l of alcoholic beverages). When crossing from North to South Cyprus, a maximum of only two packs of cigarettes may be taken across the border.

DRINKING WATER

Tap water can be drunk without reservation everywhere on the island, whether in the south or the north.

ELECTRICITY

220/240 Volt AC. Most hotel receptions provide adapters, if required, but to be on the safe side, visitors from the UK should bring a three-to-two pin adapter,

North Americans one for their two-pin to European two-round pin.

EMERGENCY

South Cyprus: police, fire service, ambulance: tel. 112 or 199
North Cyprus: police tel. 155, ambulance tel. 112, fire service tel. 199

HEALTH

The health services on Cyprus are good. Many doctors speak English. Medical treatment and medication have to be paid right away and in cash; make sure to take out a travel health insurance policy.

HOSTELS

There are some very basic youth hostels (requiring an International Youth Hostel Membership Card) in Lárnaka, Nicosia, Páfos, Stavrós tis Psókas and Tróodos.

IMMIGRATION

Citizens from the British Isles and the US need a valid passport.

INFORMATION

TOURIST BOARD – CYPRUS
– 17 Hanover Street | Mayfair | London W1S 1YP | UK | tel. +44 20 75 69 88 00 | www.visitcyprus.com
– 13 East 40th Street | New York | NY 10016-0110 | US | tel. +1 212 683 5280 | www.visitcyprus.com

NORTHERN CYPRUS TOURISM CENTRE
www.northcyprusonline.com or *www.cypnet.co.uk*

LANGUAGE & SCRIPT

Most Cypriots speak good English, with the exception of immigrants from the Turkish mainland to northern Cyprus. The Greeks are proud of their unique script. Vowels with an accent are stressed. Signs in towns often include our Latin script. What is problematic is the transcription of Greek letters; there is no uniform rule. This guide uses a modern notation designed to facilitate pronunciation and recognition on your travels. However, you may well come across different spellings.

AGRITOURISM

In all parts of South Cyprus there are small guesthouses, hotels and apartment complexes in the countryside, far away from mass tourism. The owners are usually local families and a lot of accommodation has been established in historic houses. Often a breakfast with regional products is served and sometimes it's possible to take part in agricultural activities. Meals are taken in local tavernas and those renting a flat can nearly always get eggs and vegetables from their neighbours. The accommodation listings of the Cyprus tourist board include these options under 'Traditional Houses & Flats' and some 60 places to stay in the countryside can be found on the website of the official agritourism association *www.agrotourism.com.cy*.

NEWSPAPERS, RADIO & TV

Newspapers and magazines are available one day after publication. In southern Cyprus, you also have the English daily newspaper 'Cyprus Mail', as well as the 'Cyprus Weekly' newspaper. Many hotels can also receive English TV channels.

NUDISM

Full nudism is prohibited on the entire island and going topless is only tolerated in South Cyprus.

OPENING HOURS

On all of Cyprus, shops and markets are usually open Mon–Sat 8am–8pm (Oct–April to 7.30pm), Wed only until 3pm.

PHONE & MOBILE PHONE

Cypriot phone numbers have eight digits in the south, seven in the north, and have to be dialled in full even when only making a local call. The best option is to use the numerous phone cards available. These are sold at kiosks and in supermarkets.

Phone calls between northern and southern Cyprus are considered international calls. To dial the north from abroad (and the south), dial *0090392*, for the south *00357*.

If you're planning to use your mobile phone a lot or even just to receive text messages and incoming calls, you are better off buying a Cypriot SIM card with local phone number in one of the many mobile/cell phone shops. The costs usually stay below the 10-euro mark, and your phone can be unlocked right away. You will, however, have to show your passport. Dialling codes: *UK 0044 | ROI 00353 | US/CAN 001*

PHOTOGRAPHY & FILMING

There is no charge for taking pictures and film footage at archaeological sites. At state-run museums you have to apply for permission in advance, in writing. Taking photographs or videoing military installations, including the Green Line in Nicosia, is strictly prohibited.

Almond blossom on Cyprus

POST

In southern Cyprus post offices are open Mon–Fri 7.30am–1pm, Sat 7.30am–noon, with the main post offices in the cities offering additional opening hours of Mon–Fri 4pm–6pm. Opening times in northern Cyprus: Mon–Fri 8am–1pm and 2pm–5pm, Sat 9am–noon.

PRICES & CURRENCY

On 1 January, 2008, the euro replaced the Cypriot currency, the lira (also called pound). While the lira is the official currency in the north, euros are gladly accepted there. Traveller Cheques are redeemed by all banks. Credit cards are widely used.

The cost of living in southern Cyprus is similar to Western Europe, with the exception of petrol, which is noticeably cheaper. In northern Cyprus living costs are some 10 per cent lower.

PUBLIC TRANSPORT

The cheapest way to get around is by coach. Buses connect all towns and cities within the relevant part of the island. Many villages are not so easy to reach by bus, as the buses head into the towns and cities in the morning and only in the afternoon back to the villages. An alternative are collective taxis (Service Taxis), usually with seven seats, which ply the same routes. You book a seat over the phone, will be collected at any address and taken to any address at your destination. Buses and collective taxis only operate during the day, buses also nearly always only on weekdays. On Sundays, there are far fewer collective taxis available. Individual taxis are fitted with taximeters. For the trip from Lárnaka airport to Nicosia you'll pay approx. 60 euros between 6am and 8.30pm, for the drive from northern Nicosia to Kerýneia /Girne 30 euros.

CURRENCY CONVERTER

£	€	€	£
1	1.10	1	0.90
3	3.30	3	2.70
5	5.50	5	4.50
13	14.30	13	11.70
40	44	40	36
75	82.50	75	67.50
120	132	120	108
250	275	250	225
500	550	500	450

$	€	€	$
1	0.70	1	1.40
3	2.10	3	4.20
5	3.50	5	7
13	9.10	13	18.20
40	28	40	56
75	52.50	75	105
120	84	120	168
250	175	250	350
500	350	500	700

For current exchange rates see www.xe.com

SIGHTSEEING TOURS

Organised tours with a guide are available in all Cypriot towns and tourist resorts. The island's modest size means that nearly all destinations can be reached on a day trip. While day trips into the north of the island, departing from South Cyprus, are arranged with Greek-Cypriot tour guides, this is not possible vice versa. Within the towns and villages of the South, the local offices of the Cyprus tourist board also offer free guided tours several times a week.

SMOKING

The whole of Cyprus has strict non-smoking laws banning smoking in public spaces, offices and on all means of transport.

TIME DIFFERENCE

Cyprus is two hours ahead of the UK and ROI all year round.

TIPPING

While the bills issued by hotels and restaurants already include a service charge, if you were happy with the service, staff appreciate a tip (5–10 %).

TOILETS

In basic hotels and restaurants guests are often asked to place used toilet paper in a bucket or wastepaper basket. This is done to avoid blocking the often-narrow pipes.

TRAVELLERS WITH DISABILITIES

The British influence has turned Cyprus into one of the best destinations on the Mediterranean for those with impaired mobility. Most museums are adapted to visitors in a wheelchair, and hotels suitable for wheelchair users in southern Cyprus are flagged up in their official accommodation listing. A helpful source of information is *http://media.visitcyprus. com/media/eBrochures/High/Info_for_ Disabled_feb10_lrg.pdf*. One tour operator specialising in Cyprus trips for visitors with disabilities is *Voni-Touristik (www. voni-touristik.com)*.

WHEN TO GO

Cyprus is an all-year-round destination, even though between December and April only hardy folk will want to swim in the sea. Nature lovers appreciate the months of April and May for the spectacular flowers.

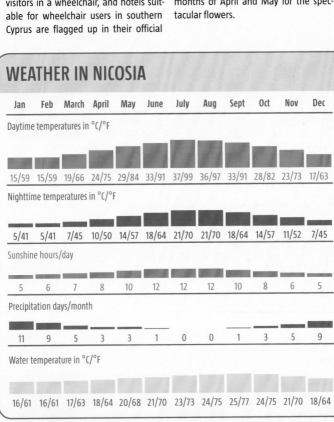

WEATHER IN NICOSIA

	Jan	Feb	March	April	May	June	July	Aug	Sept	Oct	Nov	Dec
Daytime temperatures in °C/°F	15/59	15/59	19/66	24/75	29/84	33/91	37/99	36/97	33/91	28/82	23/73	17/63
Nighttime temperatures in °C/°F	5/41	5/41	7/45	10/50	14/57	18/64	21/70	21/70	18/64	14/57	11/52	7/45
Sunshine hours/day	5	6	7	8	10	12	12	12	10	8	6	5
Precipitation days/month	11	9	5	3	3	1	0	0	1	3	5	9
Water temperature in °C/°F	16/61	16/61	17/63	18/64	20/68	21/70	23/73	24/75	25/77	24/75	21/70	18/64

USEFUL PHRASES
GREEK

PRONUNCIATION

We have provided a simple pronunciation aid for the Greek words (see middle column). Note the following:

'   the following syllable is emphasised

δ   in Greek (shown as "dh" in middle column) is like "th" in "there"

θ   in Greek (shown as "th" in middle column) is like "th" in "think"

Χ   in Greek (shown as "ch" in middle column) is like a rough "h" or "ch" in Scottish "loch"

Α	α	a	Η	η	i	Ν	ν	n	Τ	τ	t
Β	β	v	Θ	θ	th	Ξ	ξ	ks, x	Υ	υ	i, y
Γ	γ	g, y	Ι	ι	i, y	Ο	ο	o	Φ	φ	f
Δ	δ	th	Κ	κ	k	Π	π	p	Χ	χ	ch
Ε	ε	e	Λ	λ	l	Ρ	ρ	r	Ψ	ψ	ps
Ζ	ζ	z	Μ	μ	m	Σ	σ, ς	s, ss	Ω	ω	o

IN BRIEF

Yes/No/Maybe	nä/'ochi/'issos	Ναι./ Όχι./Ίσως.
Please/Thank you	paraka'lo/äfcharis'to	Παρακαλώ./Ευχαριστώ.
Sorry	sig'nomi	Συγνώμη!
Excuse me	mä sig'chorite	Με συγχωρείτε!
May I ...?	äpi'träppäte ...?	Επιτρέπεται ...?
Pardon?	o'riste?	Ορίστε?
I would like to .../	'thälo .../	Θέλω .../
have you got ...?	'ächäte ...?	Έχετε ...?
How much is ...?	'posso 'kani ...?	Πόσο κάνει ...?
I (don't) like this	Af'to (dhän) mu a'rässi	Αυτό (δεν) μου αρέσει.
good/bad	ka'llo/kak'ko	καλό/κακό
too much/much/little	'para pol'li/pol'li/'ligo	πάρα πολύ/πολύ/λίγο
everything/nothing	ólla/'tipottal	όλα/τίποτα

GREETINGS, FAREWELL

Good morning!/after-noon!/evening!/night!	kalli'mera/kalli'mera!/kalli'spera!/kalli'nichta!	Καλημέρα/Καλημέρα!/Καλησπέρα!/Καληνύχτα!
Hello!/goodbye!	'ya (su/sass)!/a'dio!/ya (su/sass)!	Γεία (σου/σας)!/αντίο!/Γεία (σου/σας)!
My name is ...	me 'lene ...	Με λένε ...

Milás elliniká?

"Do you speak Greek?" This guide will help you to say the basic words and phrases in Greek.

DATE & TIME

Monday/Tuesday	dhef'tera/'triti	Δευτέρα/Τρίτη
Wednesday/Thursday	tet'tarti/'pempti	Τετάρτη/Πέμπτη
Friday/Saturday	paraske'vi/'savatto	Παρασκευή/Σάββατο
Sunday/weekday	kiria'ki/er'gassimi	Κυριακή/Εργάσιμη
today/tomorrow/yesterday	'simera/'avrio/chtess	Σήμερα/Αύριο/Χτες
What time is it?	ti 'ora 'ine?	Τι ώρα είναι;

TRAVEL

harbour	li'mani	Λιμάνι
airport	a-ero'drommio	Αεροδρόμιο
schedule/ticket	drommo'logio/issi'tirio	Δρομολόγιο/Εισιτήριο
I would like to rent ...	'thelo na nik'yasso ...	Θέλω να νοικιάσω …
a car/a bicycle/	'enna afto'kinito/'enna	ένα αυτοκίνητο/ένα
a boat	po'dhilato/'mia 'varka	ποδήλατο/μία βάρκα
petrol/gas station	venzi'nadiko	Βενζινάδικο
petrol/gas/diesel	ven'zini/'diesel	Βενζίνη/Ντίζελ

FOOD & DRINK/WHERE TO STAY

Could I please have ...?	tha 'ithella na 'echo ...?	Θα ήθελα να έχω …;
May I have the bill, please?	'thel'lo na pli'rosso parakal'lo	Θέλω να πληρώσω παρακαλώ
I have booked a room	'kratissa 'enna do'matio	Κράτησα ένα δωμάτιο
single room	mon'noklino	Μονόκλινο
double room	'diklino	Δίκλινο

SHOPPING & HEALTH

Where can I find...?	pu tha vro ...?	Που θα βρω …;
pharmacy/chemist	farma'kio/ka'tastima	Φαρμακείο/Κατάστημα καλλυντικών
bakery/market	'furnos/ago'ra	Φούρνος/Αγορά
grocery	pandopo'lio	Παντοπωλείο
doctor/dentist/paediatrician	ya'tros/odhondoya'tros/pe'dhiatros	Ιατρός/Οδοντογιατρός/Παιδίατρος
kiosk	pe'riptero	Περίπτερο
expensive/cheap/price	akri'vos/fti'nos/ti'mi	ακριβός/φτηνός/Τιμή
more/less	pio/li'gotere	πιό/λιγότερο
pain reliever/tablet	paf'siponna/'chapi	Παυσίπονο/Χάπι

USEFUL PHRASES TURKISH

PRONUNCIATION

ı	like 'a' in 'ago', e.g.: ırmak
c	like 'j' in 'jump', e.g.: cam
ç	like 'ch' in 'chat', e.g.: çan
h	like English 'h', or 'ch' in Scottish 'loch', e.g.: hamam
ğ	a silent letter than extends the vowel before it, e.g.: yağmur
j	like 's' in 'leisure', e.g.: jilet
ş	like 'sh' in 'ship', e.g.: teker
v	like 'v' in 'violin', e.g.: vermek
y	like 'y' in 'young', e.g.: yok
z	like 'z' in 'zoom', e.g.: deniz

IN BRIEF

Yes/No/Maybe	Evet/Hayır/Belki
Please/Thank you	Lütfen/Teşekkür (ederim) or Mersi
Excuse me, please!	Afedersin/Afedersiniz
May I ...?	İzin verir misiniz?
Pardon?	Efendim? Nasıl?
I would like to .../Have you got ...?	... istiyorum/... var mı?
How much is ...?	... ne kadar? Fiyatı ne?
I (don't) like that	Beğendim/Beğenmedim
good/bad	iyi/kötü
broken/doesn't work	bozuk/çalışmıyor
too much/much/little	çok fazla/çok/ az
all/nothing	hepsi/hiç
Help!/Attention!/Caution!	İmdat!/Dikkat!/Aman!
May I take a picture of you/here?	Sizin fotoğrafınızı çekebilir miyim?

GREETINGS, FAREWELL

Good morning!/afternoon!/ evening!/night!	Günaydın/İyi Günler!/ İyi Akşamlar!/İyi Geceler!
Hello! / Goodbye!	Merhaba!/Allaha ısmarladık!
See you	Hoşçakal (plural: Hoşçakalın)/ Bye bye!
My name is ...	Adım ... or İsmim ...
What's your name?	Sizin adınız ne?/Sizin isminiz ne?

Türkçe biliyormusun?

"Do you speak Turkish?" This guide will help you to say the basic words and phrases in Turkish.

DATE & TIME

Monday/Tuesday	Pazartesi/Salı
Wednesday/ Thursday	Çarşamba/Perşembe
Friday/Saturday	Cuma/Cumartesi
Sunday/working day	Pazar/İş günü
Holiday	Tatil Günü/Bayram
today/tomorrow/yesterday	bugün/yarın/dün

TRAVEL

open/closed	açık/kapalı
departure/arrival	kalkış/varış
toilets/ladies/gentlemen	tuvalet (WC)/bayan/bay
left/right	sol/sağ
straight ahead/back	ileri/geri
train station/harbour	istasyon/liman
airport	havaalanı
I would like to rent ...	... kiralamak istiyorum
a car	bir otomobil/araba
a boat/rowing boat	bir tekne/sandal
petrol/gas station	benzin istasyonu
petrol/gas / diesel	benzin/dizel

FOOD & DRINK/ACCOMMODATION

The menu, please	Menü lütfen
Could I please have ...?	... alabilir miyim lütfen?
May I have the bill, lease?	Hesap lütfen
Do you have any ... left?	Daha ... var mı?
Single bed/single room	tek yataklı/tek kişilik oda
Double bed/double room	çift yataklı/çift kişilik oda

SHOPPING

Where can I find...?	... nerede bulurum?
I'd like .../I'm looking for ...	... istiyorum/... arıyorum
pharmacy/chemist	eczane/parfümeri
baker/market	fırın/pazar
shopping centre/department store	alışveriş merkezi/bonmarşe
grocery	gıda marketi, bakkal
supermarket	süpermarket

NOTES

FOR YOUR NEXT HOLIDAY ...

MARCO POLO TRAVEL GUIDES

ALGARVE
AMSTERDAM
AUSTRALIA
BANGKOK
BARCELONA
BERLIN
BRUSSELS
BUDAPEST
CALIFORNIA
CAPE TOWN
  WINE LANDS,
  GARDEN ROUTE
COLOGNE
CORFU
GRAN CANARIA
CRETE
CUBA
CYPRUS
  NORTH AND SOUTH
DUBAI

DUBROVNIK &
  DALMATIAN COAST
EDINBURGH
EGYPT
FINLAND
FLORENCE
FLORIDA
FRENCH RIVIERA
  NICE, CANNES &
  MONACO
HONGKONG
  MACAU
IRELAND
ISRAEL
ISTANBUL
JORDAN
KOS

LAKE GARDA
LANZAROTE
LAS VEGAS
LONDON
LOS ANGELES
MADEIRA
  PORTO SANTO
MALLORCA
MALTA
  GOZO
MOROCCO
NEW YORK
NEW ZEALAND
NORWAY
PARIS
RHODES

ROME
SAN FRANCISCO
SICILY
SOUTH AFRICA
STOCKHOLM
TENERIFE
THAILAND
TURKEY
  SOUTH COAST
UNITED ARAB
  EMIRATES
VENICE
VIETNAM

MARCO POLO
With ROAD ATLAS & PULL-OUT MAP
LAKE GARDA
MONTE BALDO WITH MOUNTAIN BIKE
The cable car in Malcesine takes bikes too
"..."KISSES" IN SALÒ
..chocolate ...lucetti"
Travel with Insider Tips

MARCO POLO
With STREET ATLAS & PULL-OUT MAP
NEW YORK
MEADOWS, WILD FLOWERS AND SKYSCRAPERS
...ng is chic: the High Line in Chelsea
...FAIR ON CLOUD NINE
...ooftop bar at 230 Fifth Street
Travel with Insider Tips

MARCO POLO
With ROAD ATLAS & PULL-OUT MAP
FRENCH RIVIERA
NICE, CANNES & MONACO
SPECTACULAR GRAND CANYON DU VERDON
Breath-taking scenery that takes some beating
SNIFFING THE AIR
The perfume manufacturers of Grasse
Travel with Insider Tips

www.marco-polo.com

...CO POLO
...AS & PULL-OUT MAP
...RLIN
A STUNNING ISLAND JUST FOR ART
Showcasing treasures from around the world
STAY COOL AT NIGHT
...scene sets the trend
Travel with Insider Tips

MARCO POLO
With ROAD ATLAS & PULL-OUT MAP
...ALLORCA
...AN FLAIR IN THE MEDITERRANEAN
Mallorca's most beautiful beach
..."E...IN" CROWD MEET
...Fonda in Deià
Travel with Insider Tips

- PACKED WITH INSIDER TIPS
- BEST WALKS AND TOURS
- FULL-COLOUR PULL-OUT MAP
  AND STREET ATLAS

ROAD ATLAS

The green line ▬▬ indicates the Trips & Tours (p. 98–103)
The blue line ▬▬ indicates The perfect route (p. 30–31)

All tours are also marked on the pull-out map

Photo: Castle at Páfos harbour

Exploring Cyprus

The map on the back cover shows how the area has been sub-divided

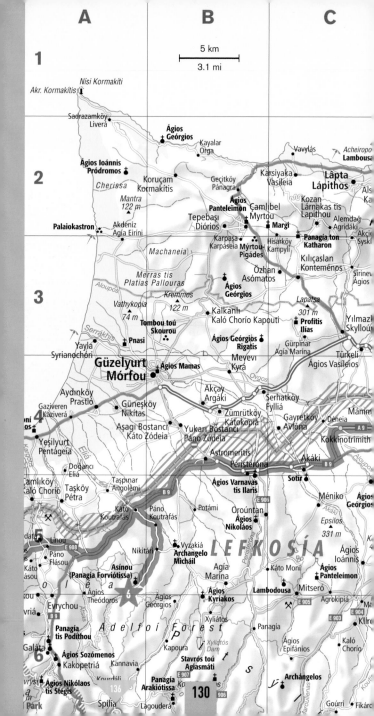

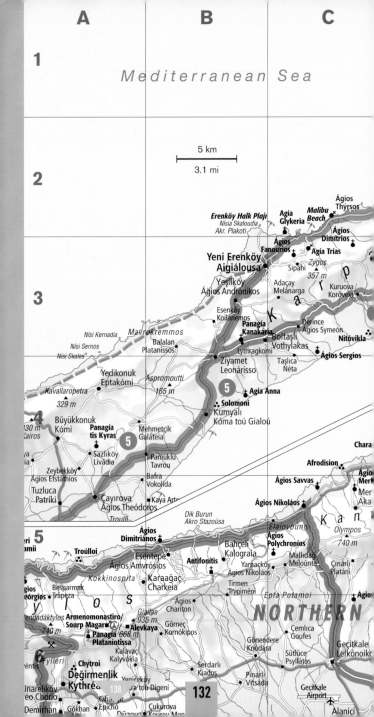

A

B

C

1

Mediterranean Sea

2

5 km

3.1 mi

Erenköy Halk Plajı **Agia** **Malibu** **Ágios**
Nisia Skaloudia **Glykeria** **Beach** **Thýrsos**
Akr. Plakoti

Ágios
Fanoúrios **Agia Triás** **Ágios**
Dimitrios

Yeni Erenköy Sipahi *Zygos*
Aigiálousa Adaçay *357 m*
Melánarga Kuruova
Yeşilköy Korovela
Ágios Andrónikos Derince
Ágios Symeón
Esenköy Nitóvikla
Koilánemos **Panagía**
Kanakária **Ágios Sergios**
Balalan Boltaşlı
Nísi Kernadia *Mavrokremmos* Platanissos Vothylakas
Nísi Sernos Lythrangómi Taşlıca
Nísi Skales Ziyamet Néta
Leonárisso

3

Yedikonuk *Aspromoutti* **Agia Anna**
Eptakómi *165 m*
Kavalloropetra
329 m ∴**Solomoni**
Kumyalı
Büyükkonuk **Kóma toú Gialoú** **Chara**
Kómi **Panagía**
tis Kyras Mehmetçik **Afrodision** **Ágio**
Galâteia **Mer**
Sazlıköy Pamuklu **Mer**
Livâdia Tavrou **Ágios Savvas** Aka
Zeybekköy Bafra
Ágios Efstáthios Vokolída **Ágios Nikoláos**
Tuzluca Çayırova *Dik Burun* K a n
Patríki Ágios Theódoros *Akro Stazoúsa*
Troúlli *Elaiovouno*
4

Ágios **Ágios** *Olympos*
Dimitriános **Polychronios** *740 m*
Troúlloi **Ágios**
Esentepe Bahçeli **Polychronios**
Ágios Amvrósios Kalograia Malldağ **Ágios**
Kokkinospria **Antifonitis** Meloúnta Çınarlı
Karaağaç Yarnacköy Platáni
5 Charkeia Ágios Nikoláos
Tirmen *Eptá Potamoí*
Trypiméni **Ágios**
Ágios **NORTHERN**
Chariton
Giálias Çemlica
Armenomonástiro/ *935 m* Göfnéç Goufes Gecitkale
Sourp Magar **Alevkaya** Görneç Lefkónoikt
Panagía *668 m* Kornókipos Gönendere
Plataniotissa Knódara Sütlüce
Kalaváç Psyllátos
Kalyvákia
Chytroi Serdarlı Pınarlı Gecitkale
Kythréa Kiados Vitsáda Airport
Cihacayır
Epichó Çukurova Alanici
Gökhan

132

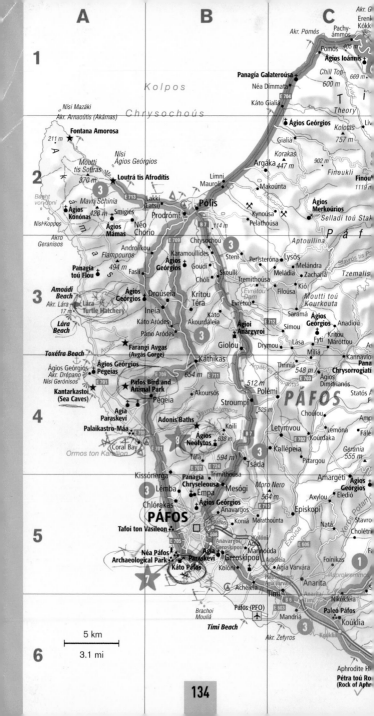

Evrychou
Ágios Theódoros
Ágios Georgios
Ágios Kyriakos
Lamboúsa
Agrokipiá

Panagía tis Podíthou
Ágios Sozómenos
Kakopetriá
Kánnavia
Adelfoí Forest
Panagía
Xyliátos
Xyliátos Dam
Panagía
Ágios Epifánios
Kaló Chorió
Klírou
E 905
E 904
E 903

Kapoura
Koutellorotsos
Stavrós toú Agiasmáti
Archángelos
Goúrri
Fikárdou
Lazaniás

Ágios Nikólaos tis Stégis
Kourdalí
Panagía Arakiótissa
1266 m
E 906
E 907

Spília
Lagouderá
Livádia
Platanistása
Ffterikoúdi
Aplíki
Palaichóri Dam
E 904
Par
Ma

1724 m
Karvoúnas
Chandriá
Polýstypos
Platýs
Álona
Askás
Palaichóri
Panagía Chryso-Pantanássa
Kámpi
Farmakás
Machairá
423
Táti

Páno Amiandos
Kyperoúnta
Agridiá
1420 m
E 923
Ágios Ioánnis
Papoútsa
1554 m

Káto Amiantos
Dymes
Agrós
Káto Mylos
1180 m
Ágios Theódoros
Odoú
Ágio Váva

Tróodos
Potamítissa
Peléndri
E 801
Tímios Stavrós
E 806

Mésa Potamos
873 m
Ágios Pávlos
Ágios Konstantínos
Sykópetra
Melíni
Or

668 m
884 m
941 m
Zoopigí
Mesevoúnos
Eptagóneia

Kouka
Ágios Geórgios
Ágios Mámas
Ágios Mámas
Arakapás
Koúmanda
Akap

Trimíklini
Kapileió
Louvarás
Dieróna
Víkla

Láneia
Agía Paraskeví
Eloros
1001 m
690 m
Kelláki
725 m
Sani

Dóros
Limnátis
762 m
Perioch
Prastió
682 m
790 m

Monágri
Korfí
Gerása
Apesiá
Apsioú
Lemesós Forest
Amiroú
Kyparissía
692 m
Épil
488

668 m
Mathikolóni
Akroúnta

Kýra
Spitáli
Fasoúla
E 109

Alassa
476 m
Paramýtha
Palódeia
Foiníkaria
Parekklisiá

Kouris Dam
Panagía Evangelistría
Germasógeia Dam
382 m
Armenochóri
Ágios Tychón
Pýrgos
147 m
20

Polemidia Dam
B 8
Agía Filaxis
Ágios Athanásios
Germasógeia
Mouttagiáka
A 1
22
Amathoús

Agía Nápa
Páno Polemídia
K. Polemídia
Ýpsonas
27
26
25
24
E 113
Mésa Geitoniá
Ágios Tychónas Beach

Kantou
Káto Polemídia
29
28
Kastró
23

Episkopí
Erími
Ýpsonas
Zakákia

Kolóssi
Kolóssi
Tracháni
**LIMASSOL
(LEMESÓS)**

Asómatos
E 601
Tzerkézoi

**AKROTÍRI
BRITISH
MILITAIRY ZONE**
Alyki
Lady's Mile Beach

Ágios Nikólaos ton Gatón
Kolpos Akrotíriou

Akrotíri
Akrotíri

64 m
59 m
Rhodos

6
Akr. Zevgári
Akr. Gáta

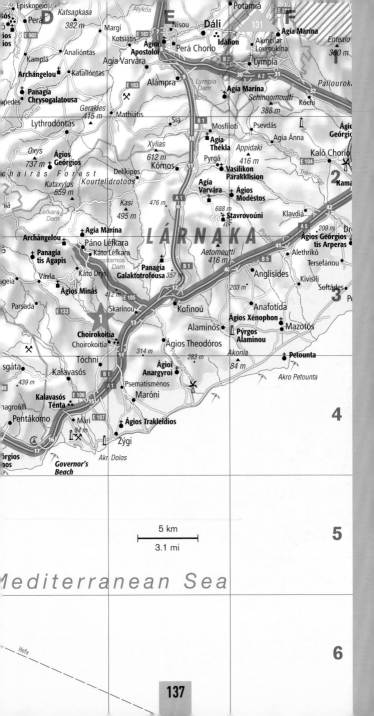

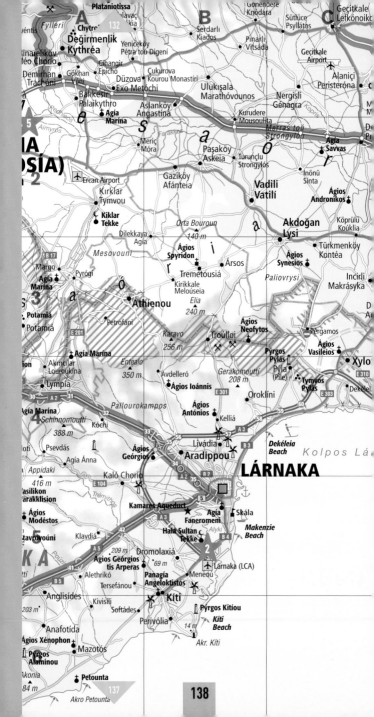

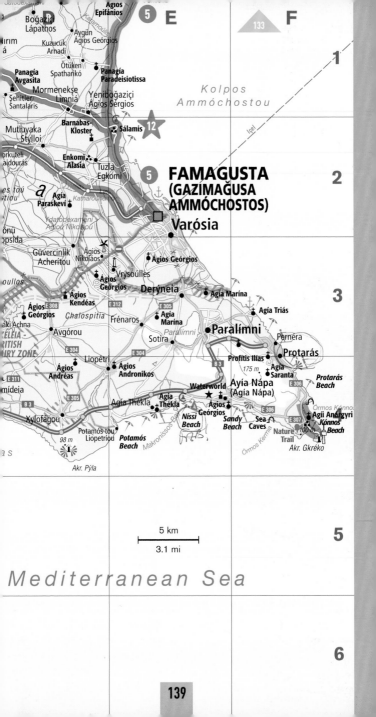

KEY TO ROAD ATLAS

A 5	Autobahn mit Nummer Motorway with number
	Schnellstraße Clearway
B 5	Fernstraße mit Nummer Highway with number
E 104	Hauptstraße mit Nummer Main road with number
	Nebenstraßen Secondary road
	Straße ungeteert Road unpaved
	Straße in Bau; in Planung Road under construction; projected
	Fahrweg Carriage way
	Distriktgrenze District border
	Sperrgebiet Prohibited area
	Nationalpark, Naturreservat National park, nature reserve
	UN-Pufferzone UN buffer area
	Britische Militärzone British military area
	Grenzlinie in UN-Pufferzone mit Checkpoint Borderline in UN buffer area with checkpoint
	Jugendherberge Youth hostel
	Jachthafen Marina
	Ankerplatz, Hafen Anchorage, harbour
	Windsurfing Windsurfing
	Wasserski Water skiing
	Ausflüge & Touren Trips & Tours

	Burg; Burgruine Castle; castle ruin
	Schloss Palace
	Kirche; Kirchenruine Church; church ruin
	Kloster; Klosterruine Monastery; monastery ruin
	Moschee Mosque
	Turm Tower
	Leuchtturm Lighthouse
	Windräder Wind engines
	Wasserfall Cascade
★	Sehenswürdigkeit Point of interest
	Archäologische Stätte Archeological site
	Bergbau (stillgelegt) Mining (closed)
	Berggipfel; Höhenpunkt Mountain top; geodetic point
)(	Paß Pass
	Aussichtspunkt Panoramic view
	Campingplatz Camping ground
	Badestrand Beach
	Internationaler Flughafen International airport
	Flugplatz Aerodrome
	Perfekte Route Perfect route

MARCO POLO Highlight

INDEX

This index lists all places and sites featured in this guide. Numbers in bold indicate a main entry.

WRITE TO US

e-mail: info@marcopologuides.co.uk

Did you have a great holiday?
Is there something on your mind?
Whatever it is, let us know!
Whether you want to praise, alert us to errors or give us a personal tip – MARCO POLO would be pleased to hear from you.
We do everything we can to provide the very latest information for your trip.

Nevertheless, despite all of our authors' thorough research, errors can creep in. MARCO POLO does not accept any liability for this. Please contact us by e-mail or post.

MARCO POLO Travel Publishing Ltd
Pinewood, Chineham Business Park
Crockford Lane, Chineham
Basingstoke, Hampshire RG24 8AL
United Kingdom

PICTURE CREDITS
Cover Photograph: Kyrenia Harbour (Getty Images/Photodisc: Allen); Sky and Clouds (Getty Images/Photodisc: Preis)
Images: K. Bötig (1 bottom); DuMont Bildarchiv: Fabig (18/19, 20, 22, 28/29, 50, 54, 66, 92, 112, 113), Richter (7, 8, 15, 21, 24/25, 112/113); Eco Tourism Cyprus (17 bottom); Getty Images/Photodisc: Allen (1 top), Preis (1 top); R. Hackenberg (flap r., 3 bottom, 4, 6, 12/13, 30 l., 72/73, 74, 86/87, 88, 91, 97); Huber: Johanna Huber (2 centre bottom, 44/45); Laif: Barbagallo (2 top, 5), IML (85); mauritius images: AGE (37, 43), Beuthan (29, 102, 108/109), Freshfood (26 r.), Kreder (30 r.), Nägele (62/63), Pigneter (104/105), Probst (117), Rossenbach (26 l.), Torino (57, 116 bottom), World Pictures (27, 110); mauritius images/White Star: Gumm (9); Le Meridien Limassol Spa & Resort (16 centre); MH BikinCyprus Events Management (17 top); Pantheon Cultural Association: Kyriakos Achilleos (16 top); Sienna Restaurant (16 bottom); T. Stankiewicz (2 below, 3 centre, 10/11, 52/53, 61, 69, 76/77, 81, 98/99, 101, 107); T. P. Widmann (flap l., 2 M. top, 3 top, 28, 32/33, 34, 38, 40, 46, 49, 58, 64/65, 70, 78, 82, 94, 116 o., 121, 128/129)

1st Edition 2013
Worldwide Distribution: Marco Polo Travel Publishing Ltd, Pinewood, Chineham Business Park, Crockford Lane, Basingstoke, Hampshire RG24 8AL, United Kingdom. Email: sales@marcopolouk.com
© MAIRDUMONT GmbH & Co. KG, Ostfildern
Chief editors: Michaela Lienemann (concept, managing editor), Marion Zorn (concept, text editor)
Author: Klaus Bötig, editor: Christina Sothmann
Programme supervision: Ann-Katrin Kutzner, Nikolai Michaelis, Silwen Randebrock
Picture editors: Iris Kaczmarczyk, Gabriele Forst
What's hot: wunder media, Munich;
Cartography road atlas: DuMont Reisekartografie, Fürstenfeldbruck; © MAIRDUMONT, Ostfildern;
Cartography pull-out map: DuMont Reisekartografie, Fürstenfeldbruck; © MAIRDUMONT, Ostfildern
Design: milchhof : atelier, Berlin; Front cover, pull-out map cover, page 1: factor product munich
Translated from German by Kathleen Becker, Lisbon; editor of the English edition: Christopher Wynne, Bad Tölz
Prepress: BW-Medien GmbH, Leonberg
Phrase book in cooperation with Ernst Klett Sprachen GmbH, Stuttgart, Editorial by Pons Wörterbücher
All rights reserved. No part of this book may be reproduced, stored in a retrieval system or transmitted in any form or by any means (electronic, mechanical, photocopying, recording or otherwise) without prior written permission from the publisher.
Printed in Germany on non-chlorine bleached paper.

DOS & DON'TS 👆

On Cyprus too there are certain things you'd better avoid

DON'T BOTHER WITH SHORT CRUISES

Some travel agencies and tour guides put a lot of effort into persuading visitors to take a short cruise to the Holy Land or to the Pyramids of Egypt. You're better off enjoying the here and now: Cyprus has more than enough to offer, the stay in Jerusalem or Cairo is just not long enough to give any satisfaction – and the guides in Israel and Egypt are more interested in provisions for souvenir sales than in providing a qualified tour.

DO REMEMBER TO BARGAIN

In Páno Léfkara every visitor gets the impression that they are arriving at sales time. There are enormous price reductions everywhere. They are however available all year round – so don't forget to bargain.

DON'T HURT RELIGIOUS FEELINGS

Dress appropriately when sightseeing: nobody is allowed into monasteries, churches and mosques without covered shoulders and knees. Before entering a mosque shoes are taken off. And if you want to respect local customs, don't fold your hands behind your back in a church, don't point to icons or turn your back to the iconostasis when standing right next to it. When visiting monasteries also bear in mind that monks and nuns have a siesta after lunch.

DO BE AWARE OF NATIONAL SENTIMENTS

For all the new freedom of travel, over half of southern Cypriots are of the opinion that tourists shouldn't stay overnight in northern Cyprus. If you want to keep on the locals' good side, it's better not to tell everybody in the south straightaway that you have spent the night in Kerýneia or Famagusta or are planning to go there.

DO ENJOY THE LOCALS' HOSPITALITY

If you're invited to a cup of coffee, you shouldn't leave before the cup is cold and to issue a return invitation straight away is rude. It would be equally inappropriate to press a tip into the hands of a Cypriot who has helped you find your way. Take their picture instead!

DON'T BE CONNED BY 'CABARETS'

If you're looking for evening entertainment you should realise that the more than 150 Cypriot 'cabarets' are more like bordellos, where most of the women working there are from Eastern Europe – and usually not there on their own free will.

DON'T GO HIKING IN SANDALS

When you go hiking, wear proper footwear. This offers protection from thorns and the less probable case of being bitten by a snake.